Manual of Arms

Manual of Arms

Drill, Tactics, & Rifle Maintenance for Infantry Soldiers During the American Civil War

ILLUSTRATED

Rifle and Light Infantry Tactics
W J Hardee

Rules for the Management and Cleaning of the Rifle Musket
Springfield Armoury

Infantry Tactics, for the Instruction, Exercise, and Manoeuvres of the Soldier
Silas Casey

Manual of Arms
Drill, Tactics, & Rifle Maintenance for Infantry Soldiers During the American Civil War
Rifle and Light Infantry Tactics
ILLUSTRATED
by W J Hardee
Rules for the Management and Cleaning of the Rifle Musket
by Springfield Armoury
Infantry Tactics, for the Instruction, Exercise, and Manoeuvres of the Soldier
by Silas Casey

FIRST EDITION

First published under the titles
Rifle and Light Infantry Tactics
Rules for the Management and Cleaning of the Rifle Musket
and
Infantry Tactics, for the Instruction, Exercise, and Manoeuvres of the Soldierr

Leonaur is an imprint of Oakpast Ltd
Copyright in this form © 2017 Oakpast Ltd

ISBN: 978-1-78282-579-1 (hardcover)
ISBN: 978-1-78282-580-7 (softcover)

http://www.leonaur.com

Publisher's Notes
The views expressed in this book are not necessarily those of the publisher.

Contents

Rifle and Light Infantry Tactics   7

Rules for the Management and Cleaning of the
Rifle Musket,   69

Infantry Tactics, for the Instruction, Exercise, and
Manoeuvres of the Soldier   99

Rifle and Light Infantry Tactics

Contents

Article First	13
Article the Second	17
School of the Soldier	21

War Department,
March 29, 1855

The system of Tactics for Light Infantry and Riflemen, prepared under the direction of the War Department by Brevet-Lieutenant Colonel William J. Hardee, of the Cavalry, having been approved by the President, is adopted for the instruction of the troops when acting as Light Infantry or Riflemen, and, under the Act of May 12, 1820, for the observance of the Militia when so employed.

Jefferson Davis,
Secretary of War,

Article First

FORMATION OF A REGIMENT IN ORDER OF BATTLE, OR IN LINE.

1. A regiment is composed of ten companies, which will habitually be posted from right to left, in the following order: first, sixth, fourth, ninth, third, eighth, fifth, tenth, seventh, second, according to the rank of captains.

2. With a less number of companies the same principle will be observed, *viz.*: the first captain will command the right company, the second captain the left company, the third captain the right centre company, and so on.

3. The companies thus posted will be designated from right to left, *first* company, *second* company, &c. This designation will be observed in the manoeuvres.

4. The first two companies on the right, whatever their denomination, will form the *first division*; the next two companies the *second division*; and so on, to the left.

5. Each company will be divided into two equal parts, which will be designated as the first and second platoon, counting from the right; and each platoon, in like manner, will be subdivided into two sections.

6. In all exercises and manoeuvres, every regiment, or part of a regiment, composed of two or more companies, will be designated as a battalion.

7. The colour, with a guard to be hereinafter designated, will be posted on the left of the right centre battalion company. That company, and all on its right, will be denominated the *right wing* of the battalion; the remaining companies the *left wing*.

8. The formation of a regiment is in two ranks; and each company will be formed into two ranks, in the following manner: the corporals will be posted in the front rank, and on the right and left of platoons,

according to height; the tallest corporal and the tallest man will form the first file, the next two tallest men will form the second file, and so on to the last file, which will be composed of the shortest corporal and the shortest man.

9. The odd and even files, numbered as one, two, in the company, from right to left, will form groups of four men, who will be designated *comrades in battle.*

10. The distance from one rank to another will be thirteen inches, measured from the breasts of the rear rank men to the backs or knapsacks of the front rank men.

11. For manoeuvring, the companies of a battalion will always be equalized, by transferring men from the strongest to the weakest companies.

POST OF COMPANY OFFICERS, SERGEANTS AND CORPORALS.

12. The company officers and sergeants are nine in number, and will be posted in the following manner:

13. The *captain* on the right of the company, touching with the left elbow

14. The *first sergeant* in the rear rank, touching with the left elbow, and covering the captain. In the manoeuvres he will be denominated *covering sergeant,* or *right guide* of the company

15. The remaining officers and sergeants will be posted as file closers, and two paces behind the rear rank.

16. The *first lieutenant,* opposite the centre of the fourth section.

17. The *second lieutenant,* opposite the centre of the first platoon.

18. The *third lieutenant,* opposite the centre of the second platoon.

19. The *second sergeant,* opposite the second file from the left of the company. In the manoeuvres he will be designated left guide of the company.

20. The *third sergeant,* opposite the second file from the right of the second platoon.

21. The *fourth sergeant,* opposite the second file from the left of the first platoon.

22. The *fifth sergeant,* opposite the second file from the right of the first platoon.

23. In the left or tenth company of the battalion, the second sergeant will be posted in the front rank, and on the left of the battalion.

24. The corporals will be posted in the front rank, as prescribed in No. 8.

25. Absent officers and sergeants will be replaced—officers by sergeants, and sergeants by corporals. The colonel may detach a first lieutenant from one company to command another, of which both the captain and first lieutenant are absent; but this authority will give no right to a lieutenant to demand to be so detached.

Posts of Field Officers and Regimental Staff.

26. The field officers, colonel, lieutenant colonel and major, are supposed to be mounted, and on active service shall be on horseback. The adjutant, when the battalion is manoeuvring, will be on foot.

27. The colonel will take post thirty paces in rear of the file closers, and opposite the centre of the battalion. This distance will be reduced whenever there is a reduction in the front of the battalion.

28. The lieutenant colonel and the major will be opposite the centres of the right and left wings respectively, and twelve paces in rear of the file closers.

29. The adjutant and sergeant major will be opposite the right and left of the battalion, respectively, and eight paces in rear of the file closers.

30. The adjutant and sergeant major will aid the lieutenant colonel and major, respectively, in the manoeuvres.

31. The colonel, if absent, will be replaced by the lieutenant colonel, and the latter by the major. If all the field officers be absent, the senior captain will command the battalion; but if either be present, he will not call the senior captain to act as field officer, except in case of evident necessity.

32. The quartermaster, surgeon, and other staff officers, in one rank, on the left of the colonel, and three paces in his rear.

33. The quartermaster sergeant, on a line with the front rank of the field music, and two paces on the right.

Posts of Field Music and Band.

34. The buglers will be drawn up in four ranks, and posted twelve paces in rear of the file closers, the left opposite the centre of the left centre company The senior principal musician will be two paces in front of the field music, and the other two paces in the rear.

35. The regimental band, if there be one, will be drawn up in two or four ranks, according to its numbers, and posted five paces in rear of the field music, having one of the principal musicians at its head.

Colour-guard.

36. In each battalion the colour-guard will be composed of eight corporals, and posted on the left of the right centre company, of which company, for the time being, the guard will make a part.

37. The front rank will be composed of a sergeant, to be selected by the colonel, who will be called, for the time, *colour-bearer*, with the two ranking corporals, respectively, on his right and left; the rear rank will be composed of the three corporals next in rank; and the three remaining corporals will be posted in their rear, and on the line of file closers. The left guide of the colour-company, when these three last named corporals are in the rank of file closers, will be immediately on their left.

38. In battalions with less than five companies present, there will be no colour-guard, and no display of colours, except it may be at reviews.

39. The corporals for the colour-guard will be selected from those most distinguished for regularity and precision, as well in their positions under arms as in their marching. The latter advantage, and a just carriage of the person, are to be more particularly sought for in the selection of the colour-bearer.

General Guides.

40. There will be two *general* guides in each battalion, selected, for the time, by the colonel, from among the sergeants (other than first sergeants) the most distinguished for carriage under arms, and accuracy in marching.

41. These sergeants will be respectively denominated, in the manoeuvres, *right general guide*, and *left general guide*, and be posted in the line of file closers; the first in rear of the right, and the second in rear of the left flank of the battalion.

Article the Second

INSTRUCTION OF THE BATTALION.

42. Every commanding officer is responsible for the instruction of his command. He will assemble the officers together for theoretical and practical instruction as often as he may judge necessary, and when unable to attend to this duty in person, it will be discharged by the officer next in rank.

43. Captains will be held responsible for the theoretical and practical instruction of their non-commissioned officers, and the adjutant for the instruction of the non-commissioned staff. To this end, they will require these tactics to be studied and recited lesson by lesson; and when instruction is given on the ground, each non-commissioned officer, as he explains a movement, should be required to put it into practical operation.

44. The non-commissioned officers should also be practiced in giving commands. Each command, in a lesson, at the theoretical instruction, should first be given by the instructor, and then repeated, in succession, by the non-commissioned officers, so that while they become habituated to the commands, uniformity may be established in the manner of giving them.

45. In the school of the soldier, the company officers will be the instructors of the squads; but if there be not a sufficient number of company officers present, intelligent sergeants may be substituted; and two or three squads, under sergeant instructors, be superintended, at the same time, by an officer.

46. In the school of the company, the lieutenant-colonel and the major, under the colonel, will be the principal instructors substituting frequently the captain of the company, and sometimes one of the lieutenants; the substitute, as far as practicable, being one of the principals.

47. In the school of the battalion, the brigadier general may consti-

tute himself the principal instructor, frequently substituting the colonel of the battalion, sometimes the lieutenant colonel or major and twice or thrice, in the same course of instruction, each of the three senior captains. In this school, also, the substitute will always, if practicable, be superintended by the brigadier general or the colonel, or (in case of a captain being the instructor), by the lieutenant colonel or major.

48. Individual instruction being the basis of the instruction of companies, on which that of the regiment depends, and the first principles having the greatest influence upon this individual instruction, classes of recruits should be watched with the greatest care.

49. Instructors will explain, in a few clear and precise words, the movement to be executed; and not to overburden the memory of the men, they will always use the same terms to explain the same principles.

50. They should often join example to precedent, should keep up the attention of the men by an animated tone, and pass rapidly from one movement to another, as soon as that which they command has been executed in a satisfactory manner.

51. The sabre bayonet should only be fixed when required to be used, either for attack or defence; the exercises and manoeuvres will be executed without the bayonet.

52. In the movements which require the bayonet to be fixed, the chief of the battalion will cause the signal *to fix bayonet* to be sounded; at this signal the men will fix bayonets without command, and immediately replace their pieces in the position they were before the signal.

Instruction of Officers.

53. The instruction of officers can be perfected only by joining theory to practice. The colonel will often practice them in marching and in estimating distances, and he will carefully endeavour to cause them to take steps equal in length and swiftness. They will also be exercised in the double quick step.

54. The instruction of officers will include all the Titles in this system of drill, and such regulations as prescribe their duties in peace and war.

55. Every officer will make himself perfectly acquainted with the bugle signals; and should, by practice, be enabled, if necessary, to sound them. This knowledge, so necessary in general instruction, becomes of vital importance on actual service in the field.

Instruction of Sergeants.

56. As the discipline, and efficiency of a company materially depend on the conduct and character of its sergeants, they should be selected with care, and properly instructed in all the duties appertaining to their rank.

57. Their theoretical instruction should include the School of the Soldier, the School of the Company, and the Drill for Skirmishers. They should likewise know all the details of service, and the regulations prescribing their duties in garrison and in campaign.

58. The captain selects from the corporals in his company those whom he judges fit to be admitted to the theoretical instruction of the sergeants.

Instruction of Corporals.

59. Their theoretical instruction should include the School of the Soldier, and such regulations as prescribe their duties in garrison and in campaign.

60. The captain selects from his company a few privates, who may be admitted to the theoretical instruction of the corporals.

61. As the instruction of sergeants and corporals is intended principally to qualify them for the instruction of the privates, they should be taught not only to execute, but to explain intelligibly everything they may be required to teach.

Commands.

There are three kinds.

62. The command of *caution*, which is *attention*.

63. The *preparatory command*, which indicates the movement which is to be executed.

64. The command of *execution*, such as *march* or *halt*, or, in the manual of arms, the part of command which causes an execution.

65. The tone of the command should be animated, distinct, and of a loudness proportioned to the number of men under instruction.

66. The command *attention* is pronounced at the top of the voice, dwelling on the last syllable.

67. The command of *execution* will be pronounced in a tone firm and brief.

68. The commands of caution and the preparatory commands are herein distinguished by *italics*, those of execution by CAPITALS.

69. Those preparatory commands which, from their length, are dif-

ficult to be pronounced at once, must be divided into two or three parts, with an ascending progression in the tone of command, out always in such a manner that the tone of execution may be more energetic and elevated: the divisions are indicated by a hyphen. The parts of commands which are placed in a parenthesis, are not pronounced.

Rifle and Light Infantry Tactics: Title 2

School of the Soldier

General Rules and Division of the School of the Soldier.

1. The object of this school being the individual and progressive instruction of the recruits, the instructor never requires a movement to be executed until he has given an exact explanation of it; and he executes, himself, the movement which he commands, so as to join example to precept. He accustoms the recruit to take, by himself, the position which is explained—teaches him to rectify it only when required by his want of intelligence—and sees that all the movements are performed without precipitation.

2. Each movement should be understood before passing another. After they have been properly executed in the order laid down in each lesson, the instructor no longer confines himself to that order; on the contrary, he should change it, that he may judge of the intelligence of the men.

3. The instructor allows the men to rest at the end of each part of the lessons, and oftener, if he thinks proper, especially at the commencement; for this purpose, he commands REST.

4. At the command Rest, the soldier is no longer required to preserve immobility, or to remain in his place. If the instructor wishes merely to relieve the attention of the recruit, he commands, *in place*—REST; the soldier is then not required to preserve his immobility, but he always keeps one of his feet in its place.

5. When the instructor wishes to commence the instruction, he commands—ATTENTION; at this command the soldier takes his position, remains motionless, and fixes his attention.

6. The *School of the Soldier* will be divided into three parts:—the first, comprehending what ought to be taught to recruits without arms; the second the manual of arms, the loadings and firings; the third, the principles of alignment, the march by the front, the different

steps, the march by the flank, the principles of wheeling and those of change of direction; also, long marches in double quick time and the run.

7. Each part will be divided into lessons, as follows:

Part First.

Lesson 1. Position of the soldier without arms; Eyes right, left and front.

Lesson 2. Facings.

Lesson 3. Principles of the direct step in common and quick time.

Lesson 4. Principles of the direct step in double quick time and the run.

Part Second.

Lesson 1. Principles of shouldered arms.

Lesson 2. Manual of arms.

Lesson 3. To load in four times and at will.

Lesson 4. Firings, direct, oblique, by file and by rank.

Lesson 5. To fire and load, kneeling and lying.

Lesson 6. Bayonet exercise.

Part Third.

Lesson 1. Union of eight or twelve men for instruction in the principles of alignment.

Lesson 2. The direct march, the oblique march, and the different steps.

Lesson 3. The march by the flank.

Lesson 4. Principles of wheeling and change of direction.

Lesson 5. Long marches in double quick time, and the run, with arms and knapsacks

Part First.

8. This will be taught, if practicable, to one recruit at a time; but three or four may be united, when the number be great compared with that of the instructors. In this case the recruits will be placed in a single rank, at one pace from each other. In this part, the recruit will be without arms.

Lesson 1

Position of the Soldier.

9. Heels on the same line, as near each, other as the conformation

of the man will permit;

The feet turned out equally, and forming with each other something less than a right angle;
The knees straight without stiffness;
The body erect on the hips, inclining a little forward;
The shoulders square and falling equally;
The arms hanging naturally;
The elbows near the body;
The palm of the hand turned a little to the front, the little finger behind the seam of the pantaloons;
The head erect and square to the front, without constraint;
The chin near the stock, without covering it;
The eyes fixed straight to the front, and striking the ground about the distance of fifteen paces.

REMARKS ON THE POSITION OF THE SOLDIER.

Heels on the same Line;

10. Because, if one were in the rear of the other, the shoulder on that side would be thrown back, or the position of the soldier would be constrained.

Heels more or less closed;

Because, men who are knock-kneed, or who have legs with large calves, cannot, without constraint, make their heels touch while standing.

The feet equally turned out, and not forming too large an angle;

Because, if one foot were turned out more than the other, a shoulder would be deranged, and if both feet be too much turned out, it would not be practicable to incline the upper part of the body forward without rendering the whole position unsteady.

Knees extended without stiffness;

Because, if stiffened, constraint and fatigue would be unavoidable.

The body erect on the hips;

Because it gives equilibrium to the position. The instructor will observe that many recruits have the bad habit of dropping a shoulder, of drawing in a side, or of advancing a hip, particularly the right, when under arms. These are defects he will labour to correct.

The upper part of the body inclining forward;

Because, commonly, recruits are disposed to do the rev project the belly and to throw back the shoulders, when they wish to hold themselves erect, from which result great inconvenience in marching. The habit of inclining forward the upper part of the body is so important to contract, that the instructor must enforce it at the beginning, particularly with recruits who have naturally the opposite habit.

Shoulders square;

Because, if the shoulders be advanced beyond the line of the breast, and the back arched (the defect called *round-shouldered*, not uncommon with recruits,) the man cannot align himself, nor use his piece with address. It is important, then, to correct this defect, and necessary to that end that the coat should set easy about the shoulders and arm pits; but in correcting this defect, the instructor should take care that the shoulders be not thrown too much to the rear, which would cause the belly to project, and the small of the back to be curved.

The arms hanging naturally, elbows near the body, the palm of the hand a little turned to the front, the little finger behind the seam of the pantaloons;

Because these positions are equally important to the *shoulder-arms*, and to prevent the man from occupying more space in a rank than is necessary to a free use of the piece; they have, moreover, the advantage of keeping in the shoulders.

The face straight to the front, and without constraint;

Because, if there be stiffness in the latter position, it would communicate itself to the whole of the upper part of the body, embarrass its movements, and give pain and fatigue.

Eyes direct to the front;

Because, this is the surest means of maintaining the shoulders in line—an essential object, to be insisted on and attained.

11. The instructor having given the recruit the position of the soldier without arms, will now teach him the turning of the head and eyes. He will command:

1. *Eyes*—RIGHT. 2. FRONT.

12. At the word *right*, the recruit will turn the head gently, so as to bring the inner corner of the left eye in a line with the buttons of the coat, the eyes fixed on the line of the eyes of the men in, or supposed to be in, the same rank.

13. At the second command, the head will resume the direct or habitual position.

14. The movement of *Eyes*—LEFT will be executed by inverse means.

15. The instructor will take particular care that the movement of the head does not derange the squareness of the shoulders, which will

happen if the movement of the former be too sudden.

16. When the instructor shall wish the recruit to pass from the state of attention to that of ease, he will command:

REST.

17. To cause a resumption of the habitual position, the instructor will command:

1. *Attention.* 2. SQUAD.

18. At the first word, the recruit will fix his attention; at the second, he will resume the prescribed position with steadiness.

Lesson 2

Facings.

19. Facings to the right or left will be executed in one *time*, or pause. The instructor will command:

1. *Squad.* 2. *Right* (or *left*)—FACE.

20. At the second command, raise the right foot slightly, turn on the left heel, raising the toes a little, and then replace the right heel by the side of the left, and on the same line.

21. The full face to the rear (or front) will be executed in two times, or pauses. The instructor will command:

1. *Squad,* 2. *About*—FACE.

22. (*First time.*) At the word *about,* the recruit will turn on the left heel, bring the left toe to the front, carry the right foot to the rear, the hollow opposite to, and full three inches from, the left heel, the feet square to each other.

23. (*Second time.*) At the word *face,* the recruit will turn on both heels, raise the toes a little, extend the hams, face to the rear, bringing, at the same time, the right heel by the side of the left.

24. The instructor will take care that these motions do not derange the position of the body.

Lesson 3

Principles of the Direct Step.

25. The length of the direct step, or pace, in common time, will be twenty-eight inches, reckoning from heel to heel, and, in swiftness, at the rate of ninety in a minute.

26. The instructor, seeing the recruit confirmed in his position, will explain to him the principle and mechanism of this step—placing himself six or seven paces from, and facing to the recruit. He will himself execute slowly the step in the way of illustration, and then

command:

1. *Squad, forward.* 2. *Common time*, 3. MARCH.

27. At the first command, the recruit will throw the weight of the body on the right leg, without bending the left knee.

28. At the third command, he will smartly, but without a jerk, carry straight forward the left foot twenty-eight inches from the right, the sole near the ground, the ham extended, the toe a little depressed, and, as also the knee, slightly turned out; he will at the same time, throw the weight of the body forward, and plant flat the left foot, without shock, precisely at the distance where it finds itself from the right when the weight of the body is brought forward, the whole of which will now rest on the advanced foot. The recruit will next, in like manner, advance the right foot and plant it as above; the heel twenty-eight inches from the heel of the left foot, and thus continue to march without crossing the legs, or striking the one against the other, without turning the shoulders, and preserving always the face direct to the front.

29. When the instructor shall wish to arrest the march, he will command:

1. *Squad.* 2. HALT.

30. At the second command, which will be given at the instant when either foot is coming to the ground, the foot in the rear will be brought up, and planted by the side of the other, without shock.

31. The instructor will indicate, from time to time, to the recruit, the cadence of the step, by giving the command *one* at the instant of raising a foot, and *two* at the instant it ought to be planted, observing the cadence of ninety steps in a minute. This method will contribute greatly to impress upon the mind the two motions into which the step is naturally divided.

32. Common time will be employed only in the first and second parts of the School of the Soldier. As soon as the recruit has acquired steadiness, has become established in the principles of shouldered arms, and in the mechanism, length and swiftness of the step in common time, he will be practiced only in quick time, the double quick time, and the run.

33. The principles of the step in quick time are the same as for common time, but its swiftness is at the rate of one hundred and ten steps per minute.

34. The instructor wishing the squad to march in quick time, will command:

1. *Squad, forward.* 2. MARCH.

Lesson 4

Principles of the Double Quick Step.

35. The length of the double quick step is thirty-three inches, and its swiftness at the rate of one hundred and sixty-five steps per minute.

36. The instructor wishing to teach the recruits the principles and mechanism of the double quick step, will command:

1. *Double Quick Step.* 2. MARCH.

37. At the first command, the recruit will raise his hands to a level with his hips, the hands closed, the nails toward the body, the elbows to the rear.

38. At the second command, he will raise to the front his left leg bent, in order to give to the knee the greatest elevation, the part of the leg between the knee and the instep vertical, the toe depressed; he will then replace his foot in its former position; with the right leg he will then execute what has just been prescribed for the left, and the alternate movement of the legs will be continued until the command:

1. *Squad.* 2. HALT.

39. At the second command, the recruit will bring the foot which is raised by the side of the other, and dropping at the same time his hands by his side, will resume the position of the soldier without arms.

40. The instructor placing himself seven or eight paces from, and facing the recruit, will indicate the cadence by the commands, one and two, given alternately at the instant each foot should be brought to the ground, which at first will be in common time, but its rapidity will be gradually augmented.

41. The recruit being sufficiently established in the principles of this step, the instructor will command:

1. *Squad, forward.* 2. *Double quick.* 3. MARCH.

42. At the first command, the recruit will throw the weight of his body on the right leg.

43. At the second command, he will place his arms as indicated No. 37.

44. At the third command, he will carry forward the left foot? the leg slightly bent, the knee somewhat raised—will plant his left foot, the toe first, thirty-three inches from the right, and with the right foot will then execute what has just been prescribed for the left. This alternate movement of the legs will take place by throwing the weight of the body on the foot that is planted, and by allowing a natural, os-

cillatory motion to the arms.

45. The double quick step may be executed, with different degrees of swiftness. Under urgent circumstances the cadence of this step may be increased to one hundred and eighty per minute. At this rate a distance of four thousand yards would be passed over in about twenty-five minutes.

46. The recruits will be exercised also in running.

47. The principles are the same as for the double quick step, the only difference consisting in a greater degree of swiftness.

48 It is recommended in marching at double quick time, or the run, that the men should breathe as much as possible through the nose, keeping the mouth closed. Experience has proved that, by conforming to this principle, a man can pass over a much longer distance, and with less fatigue.

Part Second.

General Rules.

49. The instructor will not pass the men to this second part until they shall be well established in the position of the body, and in the manner of marching at the different steps

50. He will then unite four men, whom he will place in the same rank, elbow to elbow, and instruct them in the position of shouldered arms, as follows:

Lesson 1

Principles of Shouldered Arms.

51. The recruit being placed as explained in the first lesson of the first part, the instructor will cause him to bend the right arm slightly, and place the piece in it, in the following manner on the next page.

52. The piece in the right hand—the barrel nearly vertical and resting in the. hollow of the shoulder—the guard to the front, the arm hanging nearly at its full length near the body; the thumb and forefinger embracing the guard, the remaining fingers closed together, and grasping the swell of the stock just under the cock, which rests on the little finger.

53. Recruits are frequently seen with natural defects in the conformation of the shoulders, breast and hips. These the instructor will labour to correct in the lessons without arms, and afterwards, by steady endeavours, so that the appearance of the pieces, in the same line, may be uniform, and this without constraint to the men in their positions.

54. The instructor will have occasion to remark that recruits, on first bearing arms, are liable to derange their position by lowering the right shoulder and the right hand, or by sinking the hip and spreading out the elbows.

55. He will be careful to correct all these faults by continually rectifying the position; he will sometimes take away the piece to replace it the better; he will avoid fatiguing the recruits too much in the evening, but labour by degrees to render this position so natural and easy that they may remain in it a long time without fatigue.

56. Finally, the instructor will take great care that the piece, at a shoulder, be not carried too high nor too low: if too high, the right elbow would spread out, the soldier would occupy too much space in his rank, and the piece be made to waver; if too low, the files-would be too much closed, the soldier would not have the necessary space to handle his piece with facility, the right arm would become too much fatigued, and would draw down the shoulder

57. The instructor, before passing to the second lesson, will cause to be repeated the movements of *eyes right, left,* and *front,* and the *facings.*

Lesson 2

Manual of Arms.

58. The manual of arms will be taught to four men, placed, at first, in one rank, elbow to elbow, and afterwards in two ranks.

59. Each command will be executed in one *time* (or pause), but this time will be divided into motions, the better to make known the mechanism.

60. The rate (or swiftness) of each motion, in the manual of arms, with the exceptions herein indicated, is fixed at the ninetieth part of a minute; but, in order not to fatigue the attention, the instructor will, at first, look more particularly to the execution of the motions, without requiring a nice observance of the cadence, to which he will bring the recruits progressively, and after they shall have become a little familiarised with the handling of the piece.

61. As the motions relative to the cartridge, to the rammer, and to the fixing and unfixing of the bayonet, cannot be executed at the rate prescribed, nor even with a uniform swiftness, they will not be subjected to that cadence. The instructor will however, labour to cause these motions to be executed with promptness, and, above all, with regularity.

62. The last syllable of the command will decide the brisk execution of the first motion of each time (or pause). The commands *two*, *three*, and *four*, will decide the brisk execution of the other motions. As soon as the recruits shall well comprehend the positions of the several motions of a time, they will be taught to execute the time without resting on its different motions; the mechanism of the time will nevertheless be observed, as well to give a perfect use of the piece, as to avoid the sinking of, or slurring over, either of the motions.

63. The manual of arms will be taught in the following: progression: The instructor will command:

Support—ARMS.

One time and three motions.

64. (*First motion.*) Bring the piece, with the right hand, perpendicularly to the front and between the eyes, the barrel to the rear; seize the piece with the left hand at the lower band, raise this hand as high as the chin, and seize the piece at the same time with the right hand four inches below the cock.

65. (*Second motion.*) Turn the piece with the right hand, the barrel to the front; carry the piece to the left shoulder, and pass the fore-arm

extended on the breast between the right hand and the cock; support the cock against the left fore-am, the left hand resting on the right breast.

66. (*Third motion.*) Drop the right hand by the side.

67. When the instructor may wish to give repose in this position, he will command:

REST.

68 At this command, the recruits will bring up smartly the fight hand to the handle of the piece (small of the stock) when they will not be required to preserve silence, or steadiness of position.

69. When the instructor may wish the recruits to pass from this position to that of silence and steadiness, he will command:

1. *Attention.* 2. SQUAD.

70. At the second word, the recruits will resume the position of the third motion of *support arms*.

Shoulder—ARMS.

One time and three motions.

71. (*First motion.*) Grasp the piece with the right hand under and against the left fore-arm; seize it with the left hand at the lower band, the thumb extended; detach the piece slightly from the shoulder, the

left fore-arm along the stock.

72. (*Second motion.*) Carry the piece vertically to the right shoulder with both hands, the rammer to the front, change the position of the right hand so as to embrace the guard with the thumb and fore-finger, slip the left hand to the hight of the shoulder, the fingers extended and joined, the right arm nearly straight.

73. (*Third motion.*) Drop the left hand quickly by the side.

Present—ARMS.

One time and two motions.

74. (*First motion.*) With the right hand bring the piece erect before the centre of the body, the rammer to the front; at the same time seize the piece with the left hand halfway between the guide sight and lower band, the thumb extended along the barrel and against the stock, the fore-arm horizontal and resting against the body, the hand as high as the elbow,

75. (*Second motion.*) Grasp the small of the stock with the right hand below and against the guard.

Shoulder—ARMS.

One time and two motions.

76. (*First motion.*) Bring the piece to the right shoulder, at the same time change the position of the right hand so as to embrace the guard with the thumb and fore-finger, slip up the left hand to the height of

the shoulder, the fingers extended and joined, the right arm nearly straight.

77. (*Second motion.*) Drop the left hand quickly by the side.

Order—ARMS

One time and two motions.

78 (*First motion.*) Seize the piece briskly with the left hand near the upper band, and detach it slightly from the shoulder with the right hand; loosen the grasp of the right hand, lower the piece with the left, reseize the piece with the right hand above the lower band, the little finger in rear of the barrel, the butt about four inches from the ground, the right hand supported against the hip, drop the left hand by the side.

79. (*Second motion.*) Let the piece slip through the right hand to the ground by opening slightly the fingers, and take the position about to be described.

Position of order arm

80. The hand low, the barrel between the thumb and fore-finger extended along the stock; the other fingers extended and joined; the muzzle about two inches from the right shoulder; the rammer in front; the toe (or beak) of the butt, against, and in a line with, the toe of the right foot, the barrel perpendicular.

81. When the instructor may wish to give repose in this position, he will command:

REST.

82. At this command, the recruits will not be required to preserve silence or steadiness.

83. When the instructor may wish the recruits to pass from this position to that of silence and steadiness, he will command:

1. *Attention.* 2. SQUAD.

84. At the second word, the recruits will resume the position of order arms.

Shoulder—ARMS.

One time and two motions.

85. (*First motion.*) Raise the piece vertically with the right hand to the night of the right breast, and opposite the shoulder, the elbow close to the body; seize the piece with the left hand below the right, and drop quickly the right hand to grasp the piece at the swell of the stock, the thumb and fore-finger embracing the guard; press the piece against the shoulder with the left hand, the right arm nearly straight.

86. (*Second, motion.*) Drop the left hand quickly by the side.

LOAD IN NINE TIMES.

(Whenever the loadings and firings are to be executed, the instructor win cartridge box to be brought to the front).

1. LOAD.

One time and one motion.

87. Grasp the piece with the left hand as high as the right elbow, and bring it vertically opposite the middle of the body, shift the right hand to the upper band, place the butt between the feet, the barrel to the front; seize it with the left hand near the muzzle, which should be three inches from the body; carry the right band to the cartridge box.

2. *Handle*—CARTRIDGE.

One time and one motion.

88. Seize the cartridge with the thumb and next two fingers, and place it between the teeth.

3. *Tear*—CARTRIDGE.

One time and one motion.

89. Tear the paper to the powder, hold the cartridge upright between the thumb and first two fingers, near the top in this position place it in front of and near the muzzle—the back of the hand to the front.

4. *Charge*—CARTRIDGE.
One time and one motion.

90. Empty the powder into the barrel; disengage the ball from the paper with the right hand and the thumb and first two fingers of the left; insert it into the bore, the pointed end uppermost, and press it down with the right thumb; seize the head of the rammer with the thumb and fore-finger of the right hand, the other fingers closed, the elbows near the body.

5. *Draw*—RAMMER.
One time and three motions.

91. (*First motion.*) Half draw the rammer by extending the right arm; steady it in this position with the left thumb; grasp the rammer near the muzzle with the right hand, the little finger uppermost, the nails to the front, the thumb extended along the rammer.

92. (*Second motion.*) Clear the rammer from the pipes by again extending the arm; the rammer in the prolongation of the pipes.

93. (*Third motion.*) Turn the rammer, the little end of the rammer passing near the left shoulder; place the head of the rammer on the ball, the back of the hand to the front.

6. *Ram*—CARTRIDGE.
One time and one motion.

94. Insert the rammer as far as the right, and steady it in this position with the thumb of the left hand; seize the rammer at the small

end with the thumb and fore-finger of the right hand, the back of the hand to the front; press the ball home, the elbows near the body

7. Return—RAMMER.
One time and three motions.

95. (*First motion.*) Draw the rammer halfway out, and steady it in this position with the left thumb; grasp it near the muzzle with the right hand, the little finger uppermost, the nails to the front, the thumb along the rammer; clear the rammer from the bore by extending the arm, the nails to the front, the rammer in the prolongation of the bore.

96. (*Second motion.*) Turn the rammer, the head of the rammer passing near the left shoulder, and *insert* it in the pipes until the right hand reaches the muzzle, the nails to the front.

97. (*Third motion.*) Force the rammer home by placing the little finger of the right hand on the head of the rammer; pass the left hand down the barrel to the extent of the arm, without depressing the shoulder.

8. Prime
One time and two motions
★★★★★★

If Maynard's primer be used, the command will be, load in eight times, and the eight command will be, shoulder arms. and executed from return rammer, in one and two motions, as follows:

(*First motion.*) Raise the piece with the left hand, and take the position of shoulder arms, as indicated No. 76.

(*Second motion.*) Drop the left hand quickly by the side.

★★★★★★

98. (*First motion.*) With the left hand raise the piece till the hand is as high as the eye, grasp the small of the stock with the right hand; half face to the right; place, at the same time, the right foot behind and at right angles with the left; the hollow of the right foot against the left heel. Slip the left hand down to the lower band, the thumb along the stock, the left elbow against the body; bring the piece to the right side, the butt below the right fore-arm—the small of the stock against the body and two inches below the right breast, the barrel upwards, the muzzle on a level with the eye.

99. (*Second motion.*) Half cock with the thumb of the right hand, the fingers supported against the guard and the small of the stock— remove the old cap with one of the fingers of the right hand, and with the thumb and fore-finger of the same hand take a cap from the

pouch, place it on the nipple, and press it down with the thumb; seize the small of the stock with the right hand.

        9. *Shoulder*—ARMS.

One time and two motions.

100. (*First motion.*) Bring the piece to the right shoulder and support it there with the left hand, face to the front; bring the right heel to the side of and on a line with the left; grasp fhe piece with the right hand as indicated in the position of shoulder arms.

101. (*Second motion.*) Drop the left hand quickly by the side.

        READY.

One time and three motions.

102. (*First motion.*) Raise the piece slightly with the right hand, making a half face to the right on the left heel; carry the right foot to the rear, and place it at right angles to the left, the hollow of it opposite to, and against the left heel; grasp the piece with the left hand at the lower band and detach it slightly from the shoulder.

103 (*Second motion.*) Bring down the piece with both hands the barrel upwards, the left thumb extended along the stock the butt below the right fore-arm, the small of the stock against the body and two inches below the right breast, the muzzle as high as the eye, the left elbow against the side; place at the same time the right thumb on the head of the cock, the other fingers under and against the guard.

104. (*Third motion.*) Cock, and seize the piece at the small of the stock without deranging the position of the butt.

AIM (Front rank)

One time and one motion.

105. Raise the piece with both hands, and support the butt against the right shoulder; the left elbow down, the right as high as the shoulder; incline the head upon the butt, so that the right eye may perceive quickly the notch of the hausse, the front sight, and the object aimed at; the left eye closed, the right thumb extended along the stock, the fore-finger on the trigger.

106. When recruits are formed in two ranks to execute the firings, the front rank men will raise a little less the right elbow, in order to facilitate the aim of the rear rank men.

107. The rear rank men, in aiming, will each carry the right foot about ten inches to the right, and towards the left heel of the man next on the right, inclining the upper part of the body forward.

AIM (Front Rank)

AIM (Rear Rank)

FIRE.

One time and one motion.

108. Press the fore-finger against the trigger, fire, without lowering or turning the head, and remain in this position.

109. Instructors will be careful to observe when the men fire, that they aim at some distinct object, and that the barrel be so directed that the line of fire and the line of sight be in the same vertical plane. They will often cause the firing to be executed on ground of different inclinations, in order to accustom the men to fire at objects either above or below them.

LOAD.

One time and one motion.

110. Bring down the piece with both hands, at the same time face to the front and take the position of *load* as indicated No. 87. Each rear rank man will bring his right foot by the side of the left.

111. The men being in this position, the instructor will cause the loading to be continued by the commands and means prescribed No. 87 and following.

112. If, after firing, the instructor should not wish the recruits to reload, he will command:

Shoulder—ARMS.

One time and one motion.

113. Throw up the piece briskly with the left hand and resume the position of *shoulder arms*, at the same time face to the front, turning on the left heel, and bring the right heel on a line with the left.

114. To accustom the recruits to wait for the command *fire*, the instructor, when they are in the position of *aim*, will command

Recover—ARMS.

One time and one motion.

115. At the first part of the command, withdraw the finger from the trigger; at the command *arms*, retake the position of the third motion of *ready*.

116. The recruits being in the position of the third motion of *ready*, if the instructor should wish to bring them to a shoulder, he will command:

Shoulder—ARMS.

One time and one motion.

117. At the command *shoulder*, place the thumb upon the cock, the fore-finger on the trigger, half-cock, and seize the small of the stock with the right hand. At the command *arms*, bring up the piece briskly

to the right shoulder, and retake the position of shoulder arms.

118. The recruits being at shoulder arms, when the instructor shall wish to fix bayonets, he will command:

Fix—BAYONET.

One time and three motions.

119. (*First motion.*) Grasp the piece with the left hand at the bight of the shoulder, and detach it slightly from the shoulder with the right hand.

120. (*Second motion.*) Quit the piece with the right hand, lower it with the left hand, opposite the middle of the body, and place the butt between the feet without shock; the rammer to the rear, the barrel vertical, the muzzle three inches from the body; seize it with the right hand at the upper band, and carry the left hand, reversed to the handle of the sabre-bayonet.

121. (*Third motion.*) Draw the sabre-bayonet from the scabbard and fix it on the extremity of the barrel; seize the piece with the left hand, the arm extended, the right hand at the upper band.

Shoulder—ARMS.

One time and two motions.

122. (*First motion.*) Raise the piece with the left hand and place it against the right shoulder, the rammer to the front seize the piece at the same time with the right hand at the swell of the stock, the thumb and fore-finger embracing the guard the right arm nearly extended.

123. (*Second motion.*) Drop briskly the left hand by the side

Charge—BAYONET.

One time and two motions.

124. (*First motion.*) Raise the piece slightly with the right hand and make a half face to the right on the left heel; place the hollow of the right foot opposite to, and three inches from the left heel, the feet square; seize the piece at the same time with the left hand a little above the lower band. As shown in sketch opposite.

125. (*Second motion.*) Bring down the piece with both hands, the barrel uppermost, the left elbow against the body; seize the small of the stock, at the same time, with the right hand, which will be supported against the hip; the point of the sabre-bayonet as high as the eye.

Shoulder—ARMS.

One time and two motions.

126. (*First motion.*) Throw up the piece briskly with the left hand in facing to the front, place it against the right shoulder, the rammer

to the front; turn the right hand so as to embrace the guard, slide the left hand to the night of the shoulder, the right hand nearly extended.

127. (*Second motion.*) Drop the left hand smartly by the side.

Trail—ARMS.

One time and two motions.

128. (*First motion.*) The same as the first motion of *order arms*.

129. (*Second motion.*) Incline the muzzle slightly to the front, the butt to the rear and about four inches from the ground. The right hand supported at the hip, will so hold the piece that the rear rank men may not touch with their bayonets the men in the front rank.

Shoulder—ARMS.

130. At the command *shoulder*, raise the piece perpendicularly in the right hand, the little finger in rear of the barrel; at the command *arms*, execute what has been prescribed for the *shoulder* from the position of order arms.

Unfix—BAYONET.

One time and three motions.

131. (*First* and *second motions.*) The same as the first and second motions of *fix bayonet,* except that, at the end of the second command, the thumb of the right hand will be placed on the spring of the sabre-bayonet, and the left hand will embrace the handle of the sabre-bayonet and the barrel, the thumb extended along the blade.

132. (*Third motion.*) Press the thumb of the right hand on the spring, wrest off the sabre-bayonet, turn it to the right, the edge to the front, lower the guard until it touches the right hand, which will

seize the back and the edge of the blade between the thumb and first two fingers, the other fingers holding the piece; change the position of the hand without quitting the handle, return the sabre-bayonet to the scabbard, and seize the piece with the left hand, the arm extended.

Shoulder—ARMS.

One time and two motions.

133. (*First motion.*) The same as the first motion from *fix* bayonet, No. 122.

134. (*Second motion.*) The same as the second motion from *fix* bayonet, No. 123.

Secure—ARMS.

One time and three motions.

135. (*First motion.*) The same as the first motion of support arms, No. 133, except with the right hand seize the piece at the small of the stock.

136. (*Second motion.*) Turn the piece with both hands, the barrel to the front; bring it opposite the left shoulder, the butt against the hip, the left hand at the lower band, the thumb as high as the chin and extended on the rammer; the piece erect and detached from the shoulder, the left fore-arm against the piece.

137. (*Third motion.*) Reverse the piece, pass it under the left arm, the left hand remaining at the lower band, the thumb on the rammer to prevent it from sliding out, the little finger resting against the hip, the right hand falling at the same time by the side.

Shoulder—ARMS.
One time and three motions.

138. (*First motion.*) Raise the piece with the left hand, and seize it with the right hand at the small of the stock. The piece erect and detached from the shoulder, the butt against the hip, the left fore-arm along the piece.

139. (*Second motion.*) The same as the second motion of *shoulder arms from a support.*

140. (*Third motion.*) The same as the third motion of *shoulder arms from a support.*

Right shoulder shift—ARMS.
One time and two motions.

141 (*First motion.*) Detach the piece perpendicularly from the shoulder with the right hand, and seize it with the left, between the lower band and guide-sight, raise the piece, the left hand at the height of the shoulder and four inches from it; place, at the same time, the right hand on the butt, the beak between the first two fingers, the other two fingers under the butt plate.

142. (*Second motion.*) Quit the piece with the left hand, raise and place the piece on the right shoulder with the right hand, the lock plate upwards; let fall, at the same time, the left hand by the side. As shown overleaf.

Shoulder—ARMS.
One time and two motions.

143. (*First motion.*) Raise the piece perpendicularly by extending the right arm to its full length, the rammer to the front, at the same time seize the piece with the left hand between the lower band and guide sight.

144. (*Second motion.*) Quit the butt with the right hand, which will immediately embrace the guard, lower the piece to the position of shoulder arms, slide up the left hand to the height of the shoulder, the fingers extended and closed. Drop the left hand by the side.

145. The men being at support arms, the instructor will sometimes cause pieces to be brought to the right shoulder. To this effect, he will command:

Right shoulder shift—ARMS.

One time and two motions.

146. (*First motion.*) Seize the piece with the right hand, below and near the left fore-arm, place the left hand under the butt, the heel of the butt between the first two fingers.

147. (*Second motion.*) Turn the piece with the left hand, the lock plate upwards, carry it to the right shoulder, the left hand still holding the butt, the muzzle elevated; hold the piece in this position and place the right hand upon the butt as is prescribed No. 141, and let fall the

left hand by the side.

Support—ARMS.
One time and two motions.

148. (*First motion.*) The same as the first motion of *shoulder arms*, No. 143.

149. (*Second motion.*) Turn the piece with both hands, the barrel to the front, carry it opposite the left shoulder, slip the right hand to the small of the stock, place the left fore-arm extended on the breast as is prescribed No. 65, and let fall the right hand by the side.

Arms—AT WILL.
One time and one motion.

150. At this command, carry the piece at pleasure on either shoulder, with one or both hands, the muzzle elevated.

Shoulder—ARMS.
One time and one motion.

151. At this command, retake quickly the position of shoulder arms.

152. The recruits being at ordered arms, when the instructor shall wish to cause the pieces to be placed on the ground, he will command:

Ground—ARMS.
One time and two motions.

153. (*First motion.*) Turn the piece with the right hand, the barrel to the left; at the same time seize the cartridge box with the left hand, bend the body, advance the left foot, the heel opposite the lower band; lay the piece on the ground with the right hand, the toe of the butt on a line with the right toe, the knees slightly bent, the right heel raised.

154. (*Second motion.*) Rise up, bring the left foot by the side of the right, quit the cartridge box with the left hand, and drop the hands by the side.

Raise—ARMS.
One time and two motions.

155. (*First motion.*) Seize the cartridge box with the left hand, bend the body, advance the left foot opposite the lower band, and seize the piece with the right hand.

156. (*Second motion.*) Raise the piece, bringing the left foot by the side of the right; turn the piece with the right hand, the rammer to the front; at the same time quit the cartridge box with the left hand, and drop this hand by the side.

INSPECTION OF ARMS.

157. The recruits being at *ordered arms*, and having the sabre-bayonet in the scabbard, if the instructor wishes to cause an inspection of arms, he will command:

Inspection—ARMS.

One time and two motions.

158. (*First motion.*) Seize the piece with the left hand below and near the upper band, carry it with both hands opposite the middle of the body, the butt between the feet, the rammer to the rear, the barrel vertical, the muzzle about three inches from the body; carry the left hand reversed to the sabre bayonet, draw it from the scabbard and fix it on, the barrel; grasp the piece with the left hand below and near the upper band, seize the rammer with the thumb and fore-finger of the right hand bent, the other fingers closed.

159. (*Second motion.*) Draw the rammer as has been explained in *loading*, and let it glide to the bottom of the bore, replace the piece with the left hand opposite the right shoulder, and retake the position of *ordered arms*.

160. The instructor will then inspect in succession the piece of each recruit, in passing along the front of the rank. Each, as the instructor reaches him, will raise smartly his piece with his right hand, seize it with the left between the lower band and guide sight, the lock to the front, the left hand at the height of the chin the piece opposite to the left eye; the instructor will take it with the right hand at the handle, and, after inspecting it, will return it to the recruit, who will receive it back with the right hand and replace it in the position of *ordered arms*.

161. When the instructor shall have passed him each recruit will

retake the position prescribed at the command *inspection arms*, return the rammer, and resume the position of *ordered arms*.

162. If, instead of *inspection of arms*, the instructor should merely wish to cause bayonets to be fixed, he will command:

Fix—BAYONET.

163. Take the position indicated in No. 158, fix bayonets as has been explained, and immediately resume the position of *ordered arms*.

164. If it be the wish of the instructor, after firing, to ascertain whether the pieces have been discharged, he will command:

Spring—RAMMERS.

165. Put the rammer in the barrel as has been explained above, and immediately retake the position of *ordered arms*.

166. The instructor, for the purpose stated, can take the rammer by the small end, and spring it in the barrel, or cause each recruit to make it ring in the barrel.

167. Each recruit, after the instructor passes him, will return rammer and resume the position of *ordered arms*.

Remarks on the Manual of Arms.

168. The manual of arms frequently distorts the persons of recruits before they acquire ease and confidence in the several positions. The instructor will therefore frequently recur to elementary principles in the course of the lessons.

169. Recruits are also extremely liable to curve the sides and back, and to derange the shoulders, especially in loading. Consequently, the instructor will not cause them to dwell too long at a time in one position.

170. When, after some days of exercise in the manual of arms, the four men shall be well established in their use, the instructor will always terminate the lesson by marching the men for some time in ono rank, and at one pace apart, in common and quick time, in order to confirm them more and more in the mechanism of the step; he will also teach them to mark time and to change step; which will be executed in the following manner:

To mark time.

171. The four men marching in the direct step, the instructor will command:

1. *Mark time*. 2. MARCH.

172. At the second command, which will be given at the instant a

foot is coming to the ground, the recruits will make a semblance of marching, by bringing the heels by the side of each other, and observing the cadence of the step, by raising each foot alternately without advancing.

173. The instructor wishing the direct step to be resumed, will command:

1. *Forward.* 2. MARCH.

174. At the second command, which will be given as prescribed above, the recruits will retake the step of twenty-eight inches.

To change step.

175. The squad being in march, the instructor will command:

1. *Change step.* 2. MARCH.

176. At the second command, which will be given at the instant either foot is coming to the ground, bring the foot which is in rear by the side of that which is in front, and step off again with the foot which was in front.

To march backwards.

177. The instructor wishing the squad to march backwards, will command:

1. *Squad backward.* 2. MARCH.

178. At the second command, the recruits will step off smartly with the left foot fourteen inches to the rear, reckoning from heel to heel, and so on with the feet in succession till the command *halt*, which will always be preceded by the caution *squad*. The men will halt at this command, and bring back the foot in front by the side of the other.

179. This step will always be executed in quick time.

180. The instructor will be watchful that the recruits march straight to the rear, and that the erect position of the body and the piece be not deranged.

Lesson 3

To load in four times.

181. The object of this lesson is to prepare the recruits to load at will, and to cause them to distinguish the times which require the greatest regularity and attention, such as *charge cartridge, ram cartridge* and *prime*. It will be divided as follows:

182. The first time will be executed at the end of the command; the three others at the commands, *two, three* and *four.*

The instructor will command:

1. *Load in four times.* 2. LOAD.

183. Execute the times to include charge cartridge.

Two.

184. Execute the times to include ram cartridge.

Three.

185. Execute the times to include prime.

Four.

186. Execute the time of shoulder arms.

To load at will.

187. The instructor will next teach loading at will which will be executed as loading in four times, but continued, and without resting on either of the times. He will command:

1. *Load at will,* 2. LOAD.

188. The instructor will habituate the recruits, by degrees, to load with the greatest possible promptitude, each without regulating himself by his neighbour, and above all without waiting for him,

189. The cadence prescribed No. 60, is not applicable to loading in four times, or at will.

Lesson 4

Firings.

190. The firings are direct or oblique, and will be executed as follows:

The direct fire.

191. The instructor will give the following commands:

1. *Fire by squad.* 2. *Squad.* 3. READY 4. AIM.
5. FIRE. 6. LOAD.

192. These several commands will be executed as has been prescribed in the *Manual of Arms.* At the third command, the men will come to the position of *ready* as heretofore explained. At the fourth they will aim according to the rank in which each may find himself placed, the rear rank men inclining forward a little the upper part of the body, in order that their pieces may reach as much, beyond the front rank as possible.

193. At the sixth command they will load their pieces and return immediately to the position of *ready.*

194. The instructor will recommence the firing by the command:

1. *Squad.* 2. AIM. 3. FIRE. 4. LOAD.

195. When the instructor wishes the firing to cease, he will command:

Cease firing.

196. At this command the men will cease firing, but will load their pieces if unloaded, and afterwards bring them to a shoulder.

OBLIQUE FIRINGS.

197. The oblique firings will be executed to the right and left, and by the same command as the direct fire, with this single difference—the command *aim* will always be preceded by the caution, *right* or *left oblique.*

POSITION OF THE TWO RANKS IN THE OBLIQUE FIRE TO THE RIGHT.

198. At the command ready, the two ranks will execute what has been prescribed for the direct fire.

199. At the cautionary command, *right oblique*, the two ranks will throw back the right shoulder and look steadily at the object to be hit.

200. At the command, *aim*, each front rank man will aim to the light without deranging the feet; each rear rank man will advance the left foot about eight inches toward the right heel of the man next on the right of his file leader and aim to the right, inclining the upper part of the body forward and bending a little the left knee.

POSITION OF THE TWO RANKS IN THE OBLIQUE FIRE TO THE LEFT.

201. At the cautionary command, *left oblique*, the two ranks will throw back the left shoulder and look steadily at the object to be hit.

202. At the command, *aim*, the front rank will take aim to the left without deranging the feet; each man in the rear will advance the right foot about eight inches toward the right heel of the man next on the right of his file leader, and aim to the left, inclining the upper part of the body forward and bending a little the right knee.

203. In both cases, at the command, *load*, the men of each rank will come to the position of load as prescribed in the direct fire; the rear rank men bringing back the foot which is to the right and front by the side of the other. Each man will continue to load as if isolated.

TO FIRE BY FILE.

204. The fire by file will be executed by the two ranks, the files of which will fire successively, and without regulating on each other, except for the first fire.

205. The instructor will command:

1. *Fire by file.* 2. *Squad.* 3, READY.
4. COMMENCE FIRING.

206. At the third command, the two ranks will take the position prescribed in the direct fire.

207. At the fourth command, the file on the right will aim and fire; the rear rank man in aiming will take the position indicated No. 107.

208. The men of this file will load their pieces briskly and fire a second time; reload and fire again, and so on in continuation.

209. The second file will aim at the instant the first brings down pieces to reload, and will conform in all respects to that which has just been prescribed for the first file.

210. After the first fire, the front and rear rank men will not be required to fire at the same time.

211. Each man, after loading, will return to the position of ready, and continue the fire.

212. When the instructor wishes the fire to cease, he will command:

Cease—FIRING.

213. At this command, the men will cease firing. If they have fired they will load their pieces and bring them to a shoulder; if at the position of *ready*, they will half-cock and shoulder arms. If in the position of *aim*, they will bring down their pieces, half cock, and shoulder arms.

TO FIRE BY RANK.

214. The fire by rank will be executed by each entire rank, alternately.

215. The instructor will command:

1. *Fire by rank.* 2. *Squad.* 3. READY. 4. *Rear rank.*
5. AIM. 6. FIRE. 7. LOAD.

216. At the third command, the two ranks will take the position of *ready*, as prescribed in the direct fire.

217. At the seventh command, the rear rank will execute that which has been prescribed in the direct fire, and afterwards take the position of *ready*.

218. As soon as the instructor sees several men of the rear rank in the position of ready, he will command:

1. *Front rank.* 2. AIM. 3. FIRE. 4. LOAD.

219. At these commands, the men in the front rank will execute what has been prescribed for the rear rank, but they will not step off with right foot.

220. The instructor will recommence the firing by the rear rank, and will thus continue to alternate from rank to rank, until he shall

wish the firing to cease, when he will command, *cease firing*, which will be executed as heretofore prescribed.

Lesson 5

To fire and load kneeling.

221. In this exercise the squad will be supposed loaded and drawn up in one rank. The instruction will be given to each man individually, without times or motions, and in the following manner.

222. The instructor will command:

FIRE and LOAD KNEELING.

223. At this command, the man on the right of the squad will move forward three paces and halt; then carry the right foot to the rear and to the right of the left heel, and in a position convenient for placing the right knee upon the ground in bending the left leg; place the right knee upon the ground; lower the piece, the left fore-arm supported upon the thigh on the same side, the right hand on the small of the stock, the butt resting on the right thigh, the left hand supporting the piece near the lower band.

224. He will next move the right leg to the left around the knee supported on the ground, until this leg is nearly perpendicular to the direction of the left foot, and thus seat himself comfortably on the right heel.

225. Raise the piece with the right hand and support it with the left, holding it near the lower band, the left elbow resting on the left thigh near the knee; seize the hammer with the thumb, the fore-finger under the guard, cock and seize the piece at the small of the stock; bring the piece to the shoulder, *aim* and *fire*.

226. Bring the piece down as soon as it is fired, and support it with the left hand, the butt resting against the right thigh; carry the piece to the rear rising on the knee, the barrel downwards, the butt resting on the ground; in this position support the piece with the left hand at the upper band, draw cartridge with the right and load the piece, ramming the ball, if necessary, with both hands.

227. When loaded bring the piece to the front with the left hand, which holds it at the upper band; seize it at the same time with the right hand at the small of the stock; turn the piece, the barrel uppermost and nearly horizontal, the left elbow resting on the left thigh; half-cock, remove the old cap and prime, rise, and return to the ranks.

228. The second man will then be taught what has just been prescribed for the first, and so on through the remainder of the squad.

To FIRE AND LOAD LYING.

229. In this exercise the squad will be in one rank and loaded: the instruction will be given individually and without times or motions.

230. The instructor will command:

FIRE and LOAD LYING.

231. At this command, the man on the right of the squad will move forward three paces and halt; he will then bring his piece to an order, drop on both knees, and place himself on the ground flat on his belly In this position he will support the piece nearly horizontal with the left hand, holding it near the lower band, the butt end of the piece and the left elbow resting on the ground, the barrel uppermost; cock the piece with the right hand, and carry this hand to the small of the stock; raise the piece with both hands, press the butt against the shoulder, and resting on both elbows, *aim* and *fire*.

232. As soon as he has fired, bring the piece down and turn upon his left side, still resting on his left elbow; bring back the piece until the cock is opposite his breast, the butt end resting on the ground; take out a cartridge with the right hand; seize the small of the stock with this hand, holding the cartridge with the thumb and two first fingers; he will then throw himself on his back still holding the piece with both hands; carry the piece to the rear, place the butt between the heels, the barrel up, the muzzle elevated. In this position, charge cartridge, draw rammer ram cartridge, and return rammer.

233. When finished loading, the man will turn again upon his left side, remove the old cap and prime, then raise the piece vertically, rise, turn about, and resume his position in the ranks

234. The second man will be taught what has just been scribed for the first, and so on throughout the squad.

Lesson 6

Bayonet Exercise.

235. The bayonet exercise in this book will be confined to two movements, the *guard against infantry*, and the *guard against cavalry*. The men will be placed in one rank, with two paces interval, and being at shoulder arms, the instructor will command:

1. *Guard against Infantry.* 2. GUARD.

One time and two motions.

236. (*First motion.*) Make a half face to the right, turning on both heels, the feet square to each other; at the same time raise the piece slightly, and seize it with the left hand above and near the lower band.

237. (*Second motion.*) Carry the right foot twenty inches perpendicularly to the rear, the right heel on the prolongation of the left, the knees slightly bent, the weight of the body resting equally on both legs; lower the piece with both hands, the barrel uppermost, the left elbow against the body; seize the piece at the same time with the right hand at the small of the stock, the arms falling naturally, the point of the bayonet slightly elevated.

Shoulder—ARMS.

One time and one motion.

238. Throw up the piece with the left hand, and place it against the right shoulder, at the same time bring the right heel by the side of the left and face to the front.

1. *Guard against Cavalry.* 2. GUARD.
One time and two motions.

239. Both motions the same as for *guard against infantry*, except that the right hand will be supported against the hip, and the bayonet held at the height of the eye, as in *charge bayonet*.

Shoulder—ARMS.
One time and one motion.

240. Spring up the piece with the left hand and place it against the right shoulder, at the same time bring the right heel by the side of the left, and face to the front.

Part Third

241. When the recruits are well established in the *principles and mechanism of the step, the position of the body, and the manual of arms,* the instructor will unite eight men, at least, and twelve men, at most, in order to teach them the principles of alignment, the principles of the touch of elbows in marching to the front, the principles of the march by the flank, wheeling from a halt, wheeling in marching, and the change of direction to the side of the guide. He will place the squad in one rank elbow to elbow, and number the men from right to left.

Lesson 1

Alignments.

242. The instructor will at first teach the recruits to align themselves man by man, in order the better to make them comprehend the principles of alignment; to this end, he will command the two men on the right flank to march two paces to the front, and having aligned

them, he will caution the remainder of the squad to move up, as they may be successively called, each by his number, and align themselves successively on the line of the first two men.

243. Each recruit, as designated by his number, will turn the head and eyes to the right as prescribed in the first lesson of the first part, and will march in *quick time two paces forward*, shortening the last, so as to find himself about six inches behind the new alignment, which he ought never to pass; he will next move up steadily by steps of two or three inches, the hams extended, to the side of the man next to him on the alignment, so that, without deranging the head, the line of the eyes, or that of the shoulders, he may find himself in the exact line of his neighbour, whose elbow he will lightly touch without opening his own.

244. The instructor seeing the rank well aligned, will command:

FRONT.

245. At this, the recruits will turn eyes to the front, and remain firm.

246. Alignments to the left will be executed on the same principles.

247. When the recruits shall have thus learned to align themselves man by man, correctly, and without groping or jostling, the instructor will cause the entire rank to align itself at once by the command:

Right (or *left*)—DRESS.

248 At this, the rank, except the two men placed in advance as a basis of alignment, will move up in *quick time*, and place themselves on the new line, according to the principles prescribed No 243.

249. The instructor, placed five or six paces in front, and facing the rank, will carefully observe that the principles are followed and then pass to the flank that has served as the basis, to verify the alignment.

250. The instructor seeing the greater number of the rank aligned, will command:

FRONT.

251. The instructor may afterwards order *this* or *that* file *forward* or *back*, designating each by its number. The file or files designated, only, will slightly turn the head towards the basis, to judge how much they ought to move up or back, steadily place themselves on the line, and then turn even to the front, without a particular command to that effect.

252 Alignments to the rear will be executed on the same principles, the recruits stepping back a little beyond the line, and then dressing up according to the principles prescribed No. 243, the instructor

commanding:

Right (or *left*) *backward*—DRESS.

253. After each alignment, the instructor will examine the position of the men, and cause the rank to come to *ordered arms*, to prevent too much fatigue, and also the danger of negligence at *shouldered arms*.

Lesson 2

254. The men having learned, in the first and second parts, to march with steadiness in common time, and to take steps equal in length and swiftness, will be exercised in the third part only in *quick time, double quick time*, and the *run*; the instructor will cause them to execute successively, at these different gaits, the march to the front, the facing about in marching, the march by the flank, the wheels at a halt and in marching, and the changes of direction to the side of the guides.

255. The instructor will inform the recruits that at the command *march*, they will always move off in quick time, unless this command should be preceded by that of *double quick*.

To march to the front.

256. The rank being correctly aligned, when the instructor shall wish to cause it to march by the front, he will place a well instructed man on the right or the left, according to the side on which he may wish the guide to be, and command:

1. *Squad, forward.* 2. *Guide right* (or *left.*) 3. MARCH.

257. At the command *march*, the rank will step off smartly with the left foot; the guide will take care to march straight to the front, keeping his shoulders always in a square with that line.

258. The instructor will observe, in marching to the front, that the men touch lightly the elbow towards the side of the guide; that they do not open out the left elbow, nor the right arm; that they yield to pressure coming from the side of the guide, and resist that coming from the opposite side; that they recover by insensible degrees the slight touch of the elbow, if lost; that they maintain the head direct to the front, no matter on which side the guide may he; and if found before or behind the alignment, that the man in fault corrects himself by shortening or lengthening the step, by degrees, almost insensible.

259. The instructor will labour to cause recruits to comprehend that the alignment can only be preserved, in marching, by the regularity of the step, the touch of the elbow, and the maintenance of the

shoulders in a square with the line of direction; that if, for example, the step of some be longer than that of others, or if some march faster than others, a separation of elbows, and a loss of the alignment, would be inevitable; that if (it being required that the head should be direct to the front) they do not strictly observe the touch of elbows, it would be impossible for an individual to judge whether he marches abreast with his neighbour, or not, and whether there be not an interval between them.

260. The impulsion of the quick step having a tendency to make men too easy and free in their movements, the instructor will be careful to regulate the cadence of this step, and to habituate them to preserve always the erectness of the body, and the due length of the pace.

261. The men being well established in the principles of the direct march, the instructor will exercise them in marching obliquely The rank being in march, the instructor will command:

1. *Right* (or *left*) *oblique.* 2. MARCH.

262. At the second command, each man will make a half face to the right (or left), and will then march straight forward in the new direction. As the men no longer touch elbows, they will glance along the shoulders of the nearest files, towards the side to which they are obliquing, and will regulate their steps so that the shoulders shall always be behind that of their next neighbour on that side, and that his head shall conceal the heads of the other men in the rank. Besides this, the men should preserve the same length of pace, and the same degree of obliquity.

263. The instructor, wishing to resume the primitive direction, will command:

1. *Forward.* 2. MARCH.

264. At the second command, each man will make a half face to the left (or right), and all will then march straight to the front, conforming to the principles of the direct march.

To march to the front in double quick time.

265. When the several principles, heretofore explained, have become familiar to the recruits, and they shall be well established in the position of the body, the bearing of arms, and the mechanism, length, and swiftness of the step, the instructor will pass them from *quick* to *double quick* time, and the reverse, observing not to make them march obliquely in double quick time, till they are well established in the cadence of this step.

266. The squad being at a march in quick time, the instructor will command:

1. *Double quick.* 2. MARCH.

267. At the command *march*, which will be given when either foot is coming to the ground, the squad will step off in double quick time. The men will endeavour to follow the principles laid down in the first part of this book, and to preserve the alignment.

268. When the instructor wishes the squad to resume the step in quick time, he will command:

1. *Quick time.* 2. MARCH.

269. At the command *march*, which will be given when either foot is coming to the ground, the squad will retake the step in quick time.

270. The squad being in march, the instructor will halt it by the commands and means prescribed Nos. 29 and 30. The command *halt*, will be given an instant before the foot is ready to be placed on the ground.

271. The squad being in march in double quick time, the instructor will occasionally cause it to mark time by the commands proscribed No. 171. The men will then mark double quick time, without altering the cadence of the step. He will also cause them to pass from the direct to the oblique step, and reciprocally, conforming to what has been prescribed No. 261, and following.

272. The squad being at a halt, the instructor will cause it to march in double quick time, by preceding the command *march*, by *double quick*.

273. The instructor will endeavour to regulate well the cadence of this step.

TO FACE ABOUT IN MARCHING.

274. If the squad be marching in quick, or double quick time, and the instructor should wish to march it in retreat, he will command:

1. *Squad right about.* 2. MARCH.

275. At the command *march*, which will be given at the instant the left foot is coming to the ground, the recruit will bring this foot to the ground, and turning on it, will face to the rear; he will then place the right foot in the new direction, and step off with the left foot.

TO MARCH BACKWARDS.

276. The squad being at a halt, if the instructor should wish to march it in the back step, he will command:

1. *Squad backward.* 2. *Guide left* (or *right*). 3. MARCH.

277. The back stop will be executed by the means prescribed No. 178.

278. The instructor, in this step, will be watchful that the men do not lean on each other.

279. As the march to the front in quick time should only be executed at shouldered arms, the instructor, in order not to fatigue the men too much, and also to prevent negligence in gait and position, will halt the squad from time to time, and cause arms to be ordered.

280. In marching at *double quick time*, the men will always carry their pieces on the *right shoulder* or at a *trail*. *This rule is general.*

281. If the instructor shall wish the pieces carried at a trail, he will give the command *trail arms*, before the command *double quick*. If, on the contrary, this command be not given, the men will shift their pieces to the right shoulder at the command *double quick*. In either case, at the command halt, the men will bring their pieces to the position of *shoulder arms*. *This rule is general.*

Lesson 3

The march by the flank.

282. The rank being at a halt, and correctly aligned, the instructor will command:

1. *Squad, right*—FACE. 2. *Forward.* 3. MARCH.

283. At the last part of the first command, the rank will face to the right; the even numbered men, after facing to the right, will step quickly to the right side of the odd numbered men, the latter standing fast, so that when the movement is executed, the men will be formed into files of two men abreast.

284. At the third command, the squad will step off smartly with the left foot; the files keeping aligned, and preserving their intervals.

285. The march by the left flank will be executed by the same commands, substituting the word *left* for *right*, and by inverse means; in this case, the even numbered men, after facing to the left, will stand fast, and the odd numbered will place themselves on their left.

286. The instructor will place a well-instructed soldier by the side of the recruit who is at the head of the rank, to regulate the step, and to conduct him; and it will be enjoined on this recruit to march always elbow to elbow with the soldier.

287. The instructor will cause to be observed in the march, by the flank, the following rules:

That the step be executed according to the principles prescribed for the direct step;

Because these principles, without which men, placed elbow to elbow, in the same, rank, cannot preserve unity and harmony of movement, are of a more necessary observance in marching in file.

That the head of the man who immediately precedes, covers the heads of all who are in front;

Because it is the most certain rule by which each man may maintain himself in the exact line of the file.

288. The instructor will place himself habitually five or six paces on the flank of the rank marching in file, to watch over the execution of the principles prescribed above. He will also place himself sometimes in its rear, halt, and suffer it to pass fifteen or twenty paces, the better to see whether the men cover each other accurately.

289. When he shall wish to halt the rank, marching by the flank, and to cause it to face to the front, he will command:

1. *Squad.* 2. HALT. 3. FRONT.

290. At the second command, the rank will halt, and afterwards no man will stir, although he may have lost his distance. This prohibition is necessary, to habituate the men to a constant preservation of their distances.

291. At the third command, each man will front by facing to the loft, if marching by the right flank, and by a face to the right, if marching by the left flank. The rear rank men will at the same time move quickly into their places, so as to form the squad again into one rank.

292. When the men have become accustomed to marching by the flank, the instructor will cause them to change direction by file; for this purpose, he will command:

1. *By file left* (or *right*). 2. MARCH.

293. At the command *march*, the first file will change direction to the left (or right) in describing a small arc of a circle, and will then march straight forward; the two men of this file, in wheeling, will keep up the touch of the elbows, and the man on the side to which the wheel is made, will shorten the first three or four steps. Each file will come successively to wheel on the same spot where that which preceded it wheeled.

294. The instructor will also cause the squad to face by the right or left flank in marching, and for this purpose will command:

1. *Squad by the right* (or *left*) *flank.* 2. MARCH.

295. At the second command, which will be given a little before

either foot comes to the ground, the recruits will turn the body, plant the foot that is raised in the new direction, and step off with the other foot without altering the cadence of the step; the men will double or undouble rapidly.

296. If, in facing by the right or left flank, the squad should face to the rear, the men will come into one rank, agreeably to the principles indicated No. 291. It is to be remarked that it is the men who are in rear who always move up to form into single rank and in such manner as never to invert the order of the numbers in the rank.

297. If, when the squad has been faced to the rear, the instructor should cause it to face by the left flank, it is the even numbers who will double by moving to the left of the odd numbers; but if by the right flank, it is the odd numbers who will double to the right of the even numbers.

298. This lesson, like the preceding one, will be practiced with pieces at a shoulder; but the instructor may, to give relief by change, occasionally order *support arms*, and he will require of the recruits marching in this position, as much regularity as in the former.

The march by the flank in double quick time

299. The principles of the march by the flank in double quick time, are the same as in quick time. The instructor will give the commands prescribed No. 282, taking care always to give the command *double quick* before that of *march*.

300. He will pay the greatest attention to the cadence of the step.

301. The instructor will cause the change of direction, and the march by the flank, to be executed in double quick time, by the same commands, and according to the same principles as in quick time.

302. The instructor will cause the pieces to be carried either on the *right shoulder* or at a *trail*.

303. The instructor will sometimes march the squad by the flank, without doubling the files.

304. The principles of this march are the same as in two ranks, and it will always be executed in quick time.

305. The instructor will give the commands prescribed No. 282, but he will be careful to caution the squad not to double files.

306. The instructor will be watchful that the men do not bend their knees unequally, which would cause them to tread on the heels of the men in front, and also to lose the cadence of the step and their distances.

307. The various movements in this lesson will be executed in

single rank. In the changes of direction, the leading man will change direction without altering the length or the cadence of the step. The instructor will recall to the attention of the men, that in facing by the right or left flank in marching, they will not double, but march in one rank.

Lesson 4

Wheelings

General principles of Wheelings.

308. Wheelings are of two kinds: from halts, or on fixed pivots, and in march or on moveable pivots.

309. Wheeling on a fixed pivot takes place in passing a corps from the order in battle to the order in column, or from the latter to the former.

310. Wheels in marching take place in changes of direction in column, as often as this movement is executed to the side opposite to the guide.

311. In wheels from a halt, the pivot-man only turns in his place, without advancing or receding.

312. In the wheels in marching, the pivot takes steps of nine or eleven inches, according as the squad is marching in quick or double quick time, so as to clear the wheeling point, which is necessary, in order that the subdivisions of a column may change direction without losing their distances, as will be explained in the school of the company.

313. The man on the wheeling flank will take the full step of twenty-eight inches, or thirty-three inches, according to the gait.

Wheeling from a halt, or on a fixed pivot.

314. The rank being at a halt, the instructor will place a well instructed man on the wheeling flank to conduct it, and then command:

1. *By squad, right wheel.* 2. MARCH.

315. At the second command, the rank will step off with the left foot, turning at the same time the head a little to the left, the eyes fixed on the line of the eyes of the men to their left; the pivot-man will merely mark time in gradually turning his body, in order to conform himself to the movement of the marching flank; the man who conducts this flank will take steps of twenty-eight inches, and from the first step advance a little the left shoulder, cast his eyes from time to time along the rank and feel constantly the elbow of the next man

lightly, but never push him.

316. The other man will feel lightly the elbow of the next man towards the pivot, resist pressure coming from the opposite side, and each will conform himself to the marching flank—shortening his step according to his approximation to the pivot.

317. The instructor will make the rank wheel round the circle once or twice before halting, in order to cause the principles to be the better understood, and he will be watchful that the centre does not break.

318. He will cause the wheel to the left to be executed according to the same principles.

319. When the instructor shall wish to arrest the wheel, he will command:

1. *Squad.* 2. HALT.

320. At the second command, the rank will halt, and no man stir. The instructor, going to the flank opposite the pivot, will place the two outer men of that flank in the direction he may wish to give to the rank, without however displacing the pivot; who will conform the line of his shoulders to this direction. The instructor will take care to have between these two men, and the pivot, only the space necessary to contain the other men. He will then command:

Left (or *right*)—DRESS.

321. At this, the rank will place itself on the alignment of the two men established as the basis, in conformity with the principles prescribed.

322. The instructor will next command FRONT, which will be executed as prescribed No. 245.

REMARKS ON THE PRINCIPLES OF THE WHEEL FROM A HALT.

323. Turn a little the head towards the. marching flank, and fix the eyes on the line of the eyes of the men who are on that side;

Because, otherwise, it would be impossible for each man to regulate the length of his step so as to conform his own movement to that of the marching flank.

Touch lightly the elbow of the next man towards the pivot;
In order that the files may not open out in the wheel.

Resist pressure that comes from the side of the marching flank;

Because, if this principle be neglected, the pivot, which ought to be a fixed point, in wheels from a halt, might be pushed out of its place by pressure.

WHEELING IN MARCHING, OR ON A MOVABLE PIVOT.

324. When the recruits have been taught to execute well the wheel from a halt, they will be taught to wheel in marching.

325. To this end, the rank being in march, when the instructor shall wish to cause it to change direction to the reverse flank, (to the side opposite to the guide or pivot flank,) he will command:

    1. *Right* (or *left*) *wheel.* 2. MARCH.

326. The first command will be given when the rank is yet four paces from the wheeling point.

327. At the second command, the wheel will be executed in the same manner as from a halt, except that the touch of the elbow will remain towards the marching flank (or side of the guide) instead of the side of the actual pivot; that the pivot man, instead of merely turning in his place, will conform himself to the movement of the marching flank, feel lightly the elbow of the next man, take steps of full nine inches, and thus gain ground forward in describing a small curve so as to clear the point of the wheel. The middle of the rank will bend slightly to the rear. As soon as the movement shall commence, the man who conducts the marching flank will cast his eyes on the ground over which he will have to pass.

328. The wheel being ended, the instructor will command:

    1. *Forward.* 2. MARCH.

329. The first command will be pronounced when *four* paces are yet required to complete the change of direction.

330. At the command *march,* which will be given at the instant of completing the wheel, the man who conducts the marching flank will direct himself straight forward; the pivot-man and all the rank will retake the step of twenty-eight inches, and bring the head direct to the front.

TURNING, OR CHANGE OF DIRECTION TO THE SIDE OF THE GUIDE.

331. The change of direction to the side of the guide, in marching, will be executed us follows: The instructor will command:

    1. *Left* (or *right*) *turn.* 2. MARCH.

332. The first command will be given when the rank is yet four paces from the turning point.

333. At the command *march,* to be pronounced at the instant the rank ought to turn, the guide will face to the left (or right) in marching, and move forward in the new direction without slackening or quickening the cadence, and without shortening or lengthening the

stop. The whole rank will promptly conform itself to the new direction; to effect which, each man will advance the shoulder opposite to the guide, take the double quick step, to curry himself in the new direction, turn the head and eyes to the side of the guide, and retake the touch of the elbow on that side, in placing himself on the alignment of the guide, from whom he will take the step, and then resume the direct position of the head. Each man will thus arrive successively on the alignment.

Wheeling and changing direction to the side of the guide, in double quick time.

334. When the recruits comprehend and execute well, in quick time, the wheels at a halt and in marching, and the change of detection to the side of the guide, the instructor will cause the same movements to be repeated in double quick time.

335. These various movements will be executed by the same commands and according to the same principles as in quick time, except that the command *double quick* will precede that of *march*. In wheeling while marching, the pivot man will take steps of eleven inches, and in the changes of direction to the side of the guide, the men on the side opposite the guide must increase the gait in order to bring themselves into line.

336. The instructor, in order not to fatigue the recruits, and not to divide their attention, will cause them to execute the several movements of which this lesson is composed, first Without arms, and next, after the mechanism be well comprehended, with arms.

Lesson 5

Long marches in double quick time and the run.

337. The instructor will cause to be resumed the exercises in double quick time and the run, with arms and knapsacks.

338. He will cause long marches to be executed in double quick time, both by the front and by the flank, and by constant practice Will lead the: men to pass over a distance of five miles in sixty minutes. The pieces will be carried on either shoulder, and sometimes at a trail.

339. He will also exercise them in long marches at a run, the pieces carried at will; the men will be instructed to keep as united ae possible, without however exacting much regularity, which is impracticable.

340. The run, in actual service, will only be resorted to when it may be highly important to reach a given point with great promptitude.

To stack arms.

The men being at order arms, the instructor will command:

Stack—ARMS.

341. At this command the front rank man of every even numbered file will pass his piece before him, seizing it with the left hand near the upper band; will place the butt a little in advance of his left toe, the barrel turned towards the body, and draw the rammer slightly from its place; the front rank man of every odd numbered file will also draw the rammer slightly, and pass his piece to the man next on his left, who will seize it with the right hand near the upper band, and place the butt a little in advance of the right toe of the man next on his right, the barrel turned to the front; he will then cross the rammers of the two pieces, the rammer of the piece of the odd numbered man being inside; the rear rank man of every even file will also draw his rammer, lean his piece forward, the lock plate downwards, advance the right foot about six inches, and insert the rammer between the rammer and barrel of the piece of his front rank man; with his left hand he will place the butt of his piece on the ground, thirty-two inches in rear of, and perpendicular to, the front rank, bringing back his right foot by the side of the left; the front rank man of every even file will at the same time lean the stack to the rear, quit it with his right hand, and force all the rammers down. The stack being thus formed, the rear rank man of every odd file will pass his piece into his left hand, the barrel to the front, and inclining it forward, will rest it on the stack.

342. The men of both ranks having taken the position of the soldier without arms, the instructor will command:

1. *Break ranks.* 2. MARCH.

To resume arms.

343. Both ranks being re-formed in rear of their stacks, the instructor will command:

Take—ARMS.

344. At this command the rear rank man of every odd numbered file will withdraw his piece from the stack; the front rank man of every even file will seize his own piece with the left hand and that of the man on his right with his right hand, both above the lower band; the rear rank man of the even file will seize his piece with the right hand below the lower band; these two men will raise up the stack to loosen the rammers; the front rank man of every odd file will facilitate the disengagement of the rammers, if necessary, by drawing them out

slightly with the left hand, and will receive his piece from the hand of the man next on his left; the four men will retake the position of the soldier at order arms.

Rules for the Management and Cleaning of the Rifle Musket

Contents

Preservation of Arms in Service	73
Rules for Dismounting the Rifle Musket	90
Rules for the More Complete Dismounting of the Rifle Musket When Cleaned by an Armourer	94
Mr. Dingee's Directions for Reblacking Belts	97

Preservation of Arms in Service

The officers, non-commissioned officers, and soldiers should be instructed and practiced in the nomenclature of the arms, the manner of dismounting and mounting them, and the precautions and care required for their preservation.

Each soldier should have a screwdriver and a wiper, and each non-commissioned officer a wire tumbler-punch and a spring vice. No other implements should be used in taking arms apart or in setting them up.

In the inspection of arms, officers should attend to the qualities essential to service, rather than to a bright polish on the exterior of the arms. The arms should be inspected in the quarters at least once a month, with the barrel and lock separated from the stock.

NOMENCLATURE DESCRIPTIVE OF THE RIFLE MUSKET.

MODEL OF 1863.

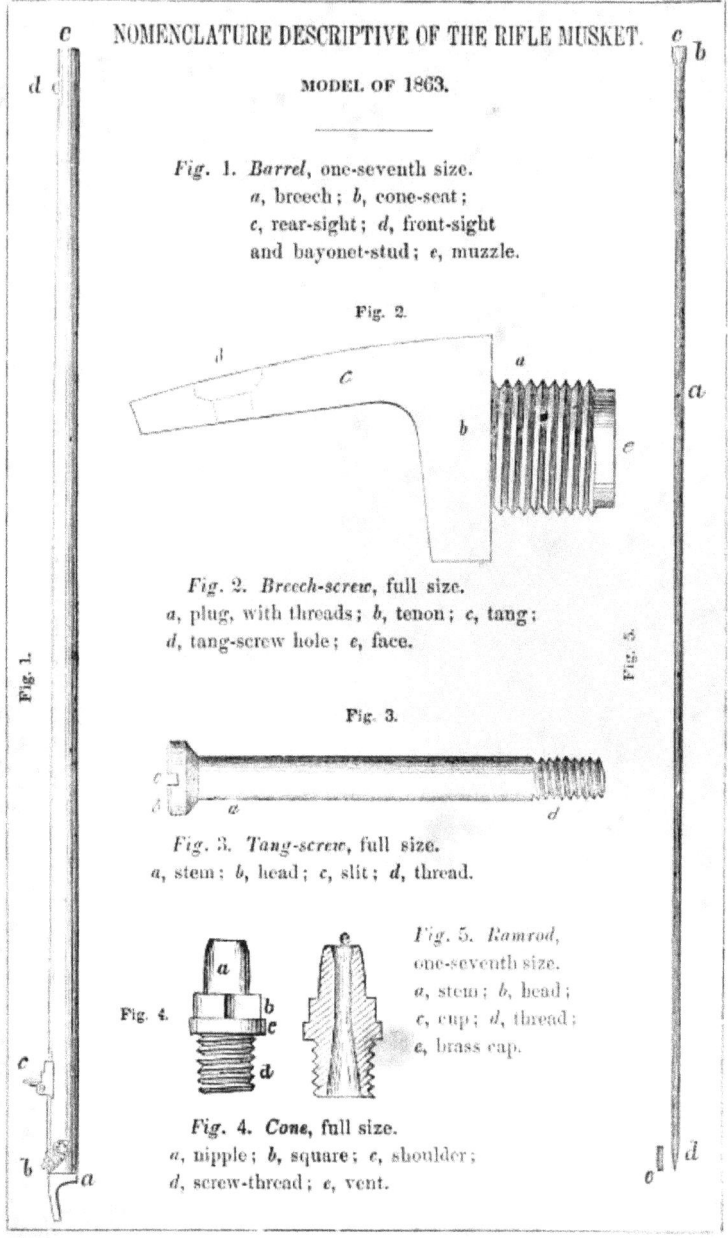

Fig. 1. **Barrel**, one-seventh size.
a, breech; *b*, cone-seat;
c, rear-sight; *d*, front-sight
and bayonet-stud; *e*, muzzle.

Fig. 2. **Breech-screw**, full size.
a, plug, with threads; *b*, tenon; *c*, tang;
d, tang-screw hole; *e*, face.

Fig. 3. **Tang-screw**, full size.
a, stem; *b*, head; *c*, slit; *d*, thread.

Fig. 5. **Ramrod**, one-seventh size.
a, stem; *b*, head;
c, cup; *d*, thread;
e, brass cap.

Fig. 4. **Cone**, full size.
a, nipple; *b*, square; *c*, shoulder;
d, screw-thread; *e*, vent.

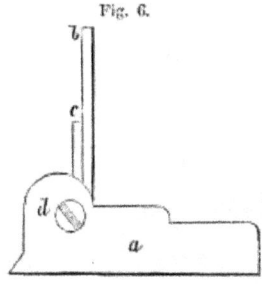

Fig. 6. *Rear-sight*, full size, side view, complete.
a, base; b, first leaf;
c, second leaf; d, screw.

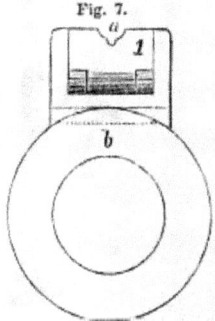

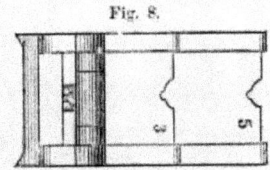

Fig. 7. *Front*, sectional view on barrel, full size.
a, notch for 100 yards range;
b, section of barrel.

Fig. 8. Top view of sight, complete, showing the graduation marks for 300 and 500 yards, and each leaf closed in the base.

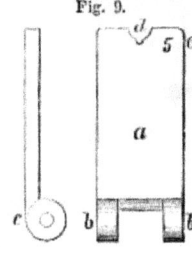

Fig. 9. *First leaf*, full size.
a, body;
b, b, ears;
c, screw-hole;
d, sight-notch;
e, graduation mark.

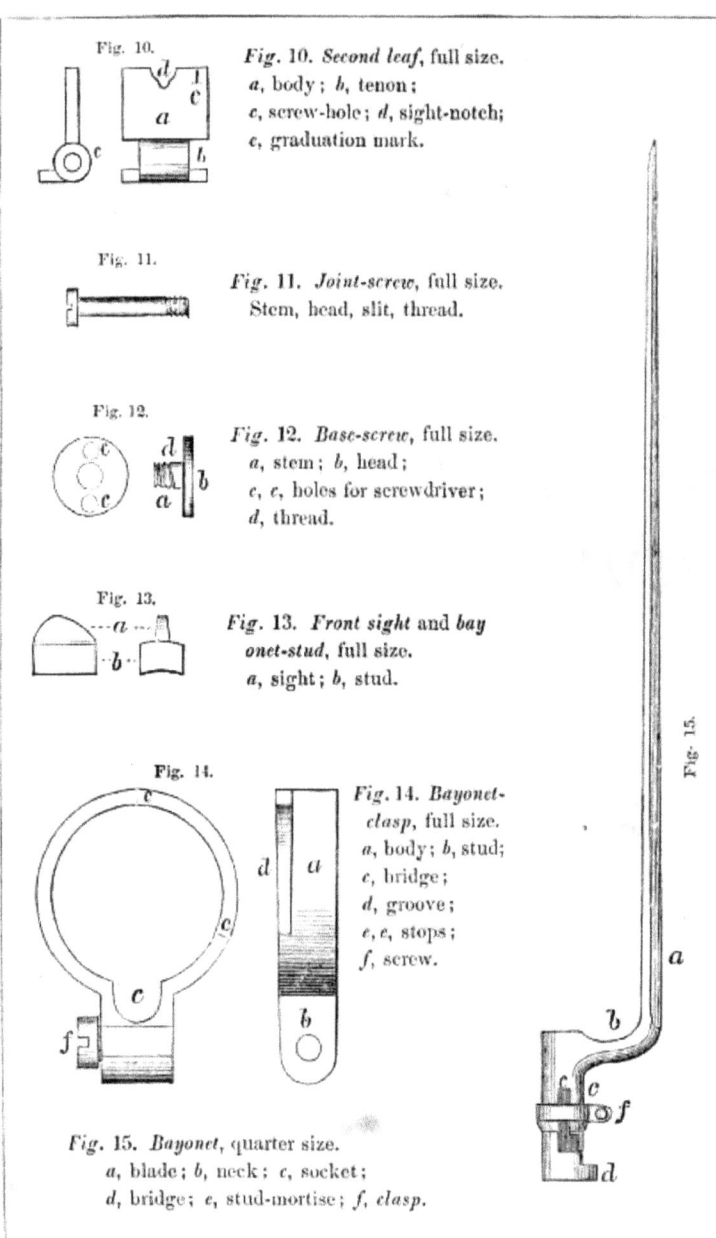

Fig. 10. *Second leaf*, full size.
  a, body; b, tenon;
  c, screw-hole; d, sight-notch;
  e, graduation mark.

Fig. 11. *Joint-screw*, full size.
  Stem, head, slit, thread.

Fig. 12. *Base-screw*, full size.
  a, stem; b, head;
  c, c, holes for screwdriver;
  d, thread.

Fig. 13. *Front sight* and *bayonet-stud*, full size.
  a, sight; b, stud.

Fig. 14. *Bayonet-clasp*, full size.
  a, body; b, stud;
  c, bridge;
  d, groove;
  e, e, stops;
  f, screw.

Fig. 15. *Bayonet*, quarter size.
  a, blade; b, neck; c, socket;
  d, bridge; e, stud-mortise; f, clasp.

Fig. 16.

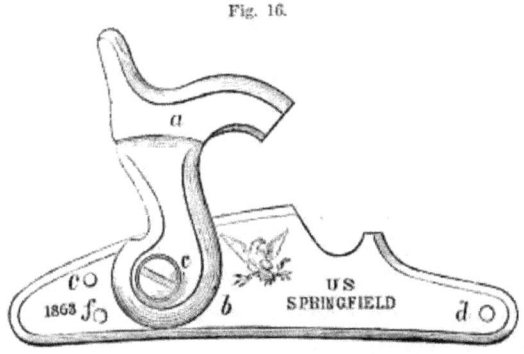

Fig. 16. *Lock,* outside view, half size.
    a, hammer; *b,* lock-plate;
    c, tumbler-screw;
    d, side-screw hole; *e,* sear-spring screw;
    f, sear screw.

Fig. 17.

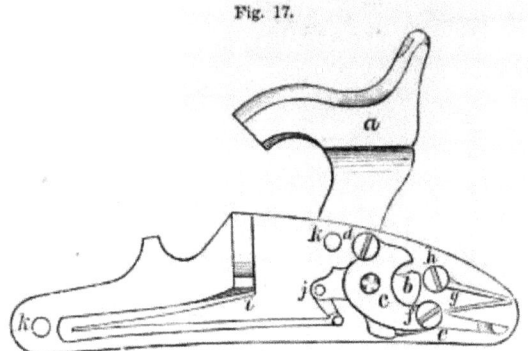

Fig. 17. *Lock,* inside view, half size, showing the parts at half-cock.
    a, hammer; *b,* tumbler; *c,* bridle;
    d, bridle-screw; *e,* sear; *f,* sear-screw;
    g, sear-spring; *h,* sear-spring screw;
    i, main-spring; *j,* swivel; *k, k,* side-screws.

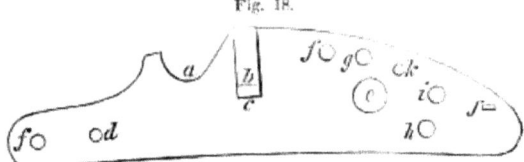

Fig. 18.

***Fig.* 18.** *Lock-plate,* half-size, showing the position of the holes, &c. *a,* cone-seat notch; *b,* bolster; *c,* main-spring notch; *d,* hole for main-spring pivot; *e,* hole for arbor of tumbler; *f, f.* side-screw holes; *g,* hole for bridle-screw; *h,* hole for sear-screw; *i,* hole for sear-spring; *j,* sear-spring stud mortise; *k,* bridle pivot hole.

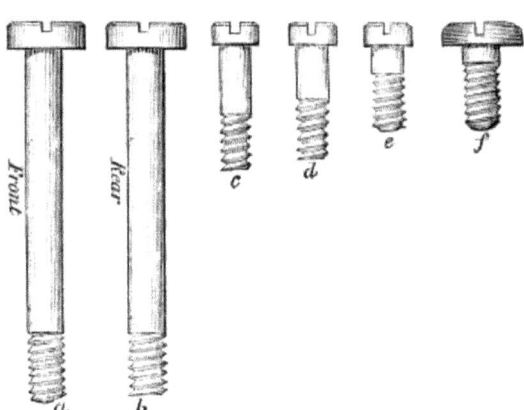

Fig. 19.

***Fig.* 19.** *Lock* and *side-screws,* full size.
    a, b, side-screws; *c,* sear-screw;
    d, bridle-screw; *e,* sear-spring screw,
    f, tumbler-screw.

Note.—In all the screws, the parts are the stem, the head, the slit, the thread.

Fig. 20.

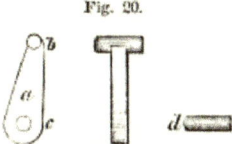

Fig. 20. Mainspring-swivel, full size.
    a, body; *b*, axis; *c*, tumbler-pin hole;
    d, tumbler-pin.

Fig. 21.

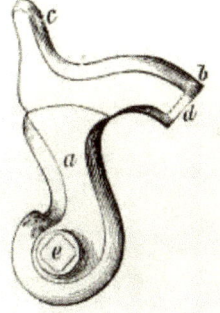

Fig. 21. Hammer, half size.
    a, body; *b*, head; *c*, comb;
    d, countersink; *e*, tumbler-hole.

Fig. 22.

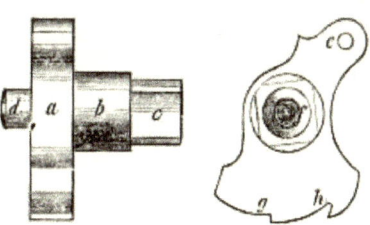

Fig. 22. Tumbler, full size.
    a, body; *b*, arbor; *c*, squares; *d*, pivot;
    e, swivel-arm and pin-hole; *f*, tumbler-screw hole;
    g, cock-notch; *h*, half-cock notch.

Fig. 23.

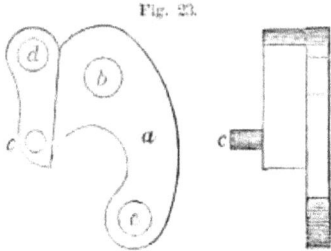

Fig. 23. *Bridle*, full size.
a, body; *b*, eye for tumbler pivot; *c*, pivot;
d, hole for bridle-screw;
e, hole for sear-screw.

Fig. 24.

Fig. 25.

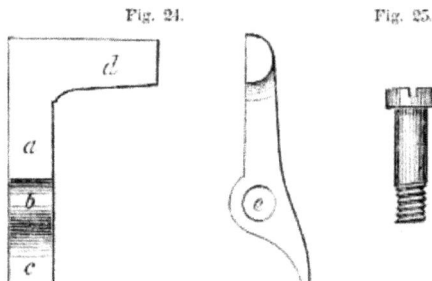

Fig. 24. *Sear*, full size.
a, body; *b*, eye; *c*, nose;
d, tang; *e*, screw-hole.

Fig. 25. *Sear-screw*, full size.

Fig. 26.

Fig. 27.

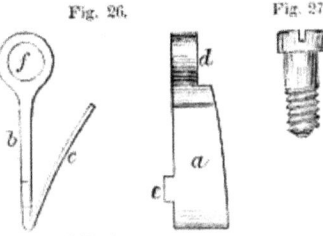

Fig. 26. ***Sear-spring***, full size.
a, blade; *b*, upper branch;
c, lower branch;
d, eye; *e*, stud; *f*, screw-hole.

Fig. 27. ***Sear-spring screw***, full size.

Fig. 28.

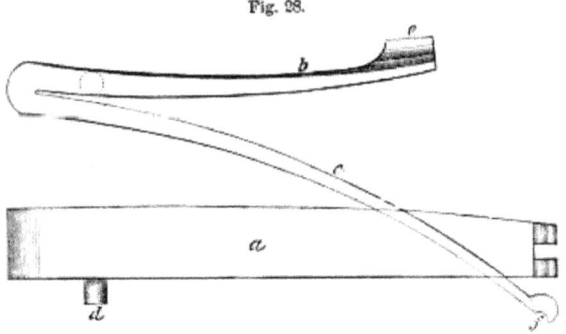

Fig. 28. ***Mainspring***, full size.
a, blade;
b, upper branch;
c, lower branch;
d, pivot;
e, tang;
f, hook.

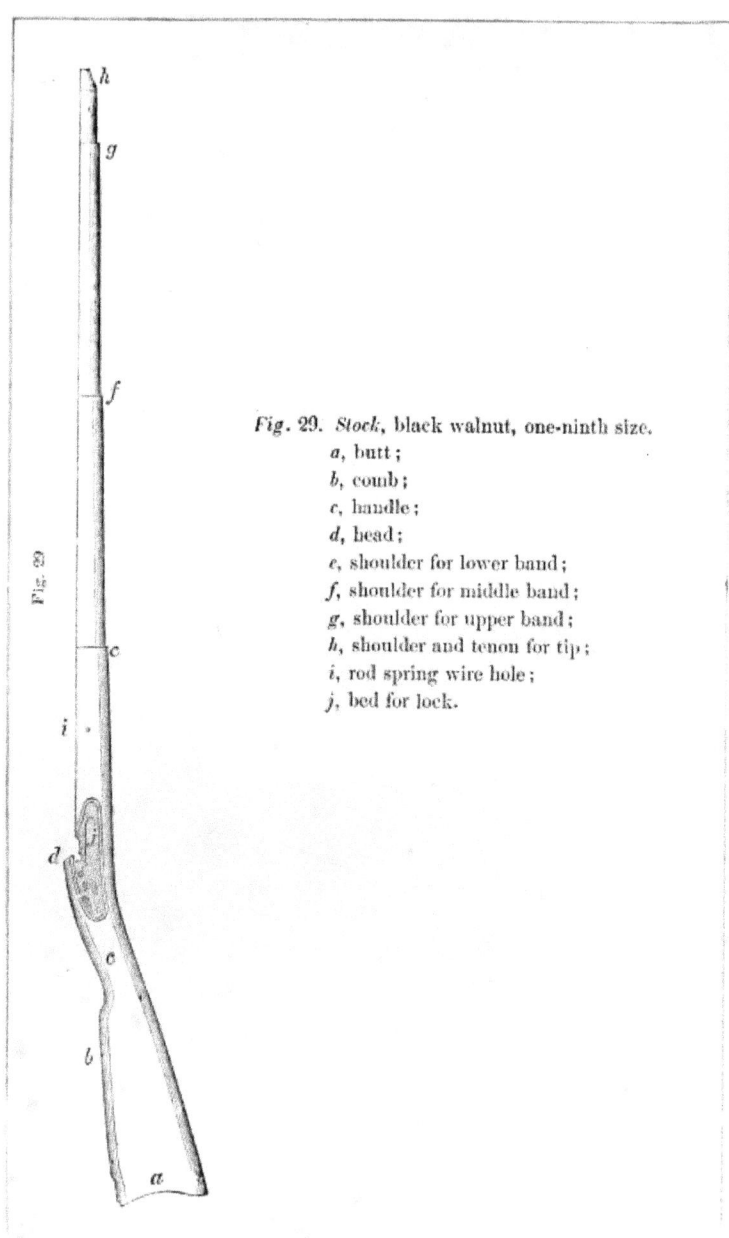

Fig. 29. *Stock*, black walnut, one-ninth size.
  a, butt;
  b, comb;
  c, handle;
  d, head;
  e, shoulder for lower band;
  f, shoulder for middle band;
  g, shoulder for upper band;
  h, shoulder and tenon for tip;
  i, rod spring wire hole;
  j, bed for lock.

Fig. 30.

Fig. 31.

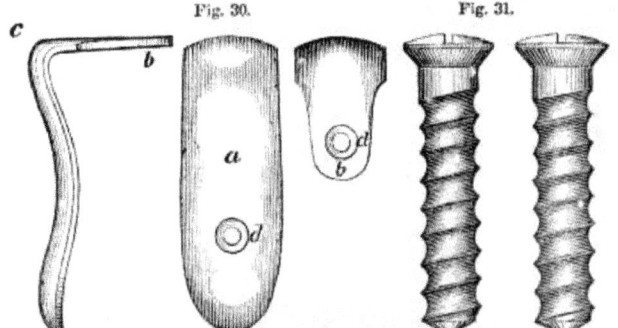

Fig. 30. *Butt-plate*, one-third size.
a, body ; *b*, toe ; *c*, heel ;
d, *d*, screw-holes.

Fig. 31. *Butt-plate screws*, full size.

Fig. 32.

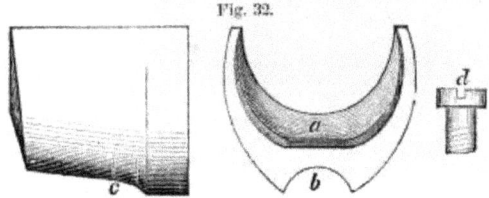

Fig. 32. *Tip*, full size, (malleable iron.)
a, recess for stock ;
b, groove for ramrod ;
c, screw-hole ;
d, screw.

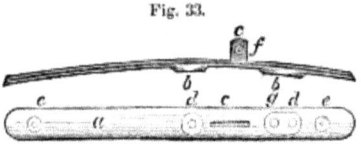

Fig. 33.

Fig. 33. *Guard-plate*, quarter size.
   a, body; *b, b*, bolsters;
   c, c, trigger-stud and mortise;
   d, d, holes for guard-bow;
   e, e, holes for wood screws;
   f, for trigger-screw; *g*, tang-screw.

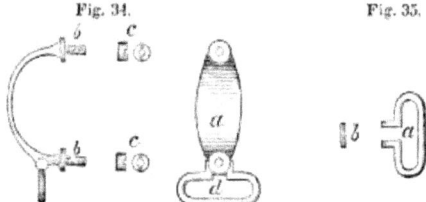

Fig. 34.   Fig. 35.

Fig. 34. *Guard-bow*, quarter size.
   a, body; *b, b*, stem; *c, c*, nuts; *d*, swivel.

Fig. 35. *Swivel*, quarter size.
   a, swivel; *b*, swivel-rivet.

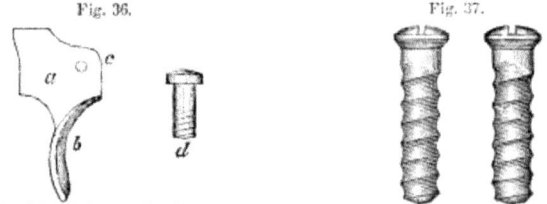

Fig. 36.   Fig. 37.

Fig. 36. *Trigger*, half size.
   a, blade; *b*, finger-piece; *c*, hole for screw;
   d, screw, full size.

Fig. 37. *Guard-screws*, full size.

Fig. 38. Fig. 39. Fig. 40.

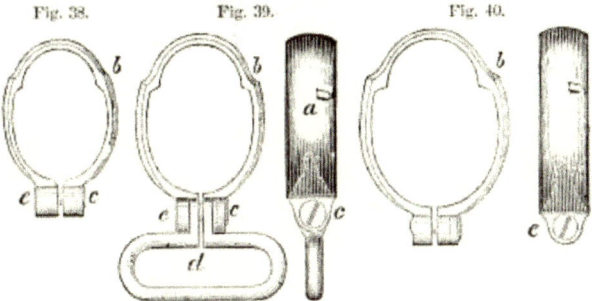

Fig. 38. *Upper band*, half size.

Fig. 39. *Middle band.*

Fig. 40. *Lower band.*
a, body ; *b*, *b*, *b*, creases ;
U, denotes the upper edge ; *c*, *c*, *c*, studs ;
d, swivel, on middle band only ; *e*, *e*, *e*, screws.

Fig. 41.

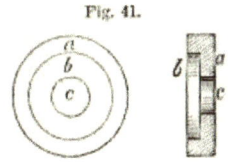

Fig. 41. *Side-screw washer*, full size.
a, body ; *b*, countersink ; *c*, hole for screw.

Fig. 42.

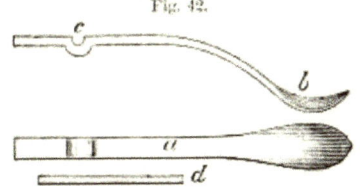

Fig. 42. *Ramrod spring*, half size.
a, blade ; *b*, groove for rod ;
c, hole for wire ; *d*, rod-spring wire.

APPENDAGES FOR RIFLE MUSKET.

MODEL OF 1863.

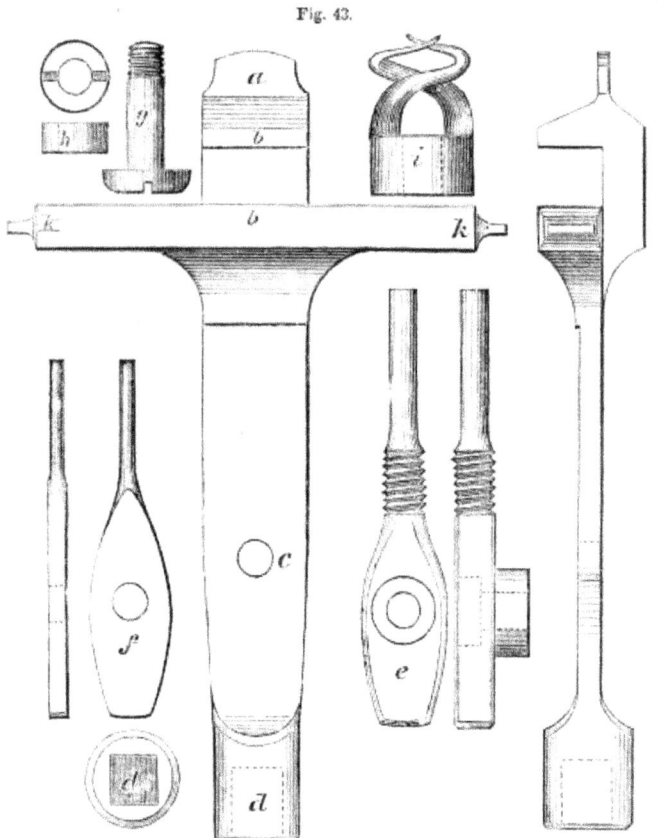

Fig. 43. *Compound appendage*, full size, embracing the vise for mainspring; cone-wrench; 3 screwdrivers; tumbler-punch; vent-wire; wiper and ball-screw, viz: *a*, screwdriver for butt, tang, and guard screws; *b, b,* mainspring vise; *c*. hole for screw; *d, d,* cone-wrench; *e*, tumbler-punch; *f*, vent-wire; *g*, screw; *h*, nut; *i*, wiper and ball-screw; *k. k,* screwdrivers for lock screws.

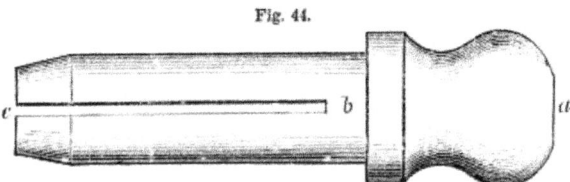

Fig. 44.

Fig. 44. *Tompion*, full size.
   a, head; *b*, body; *c*, slot.

Fig. 45.

Fig. 45. *Cone*, full size, (spare.)
   a, nipple; *b*, square; *c*, shoulder;
   d, screw-thread; *e*, vent.

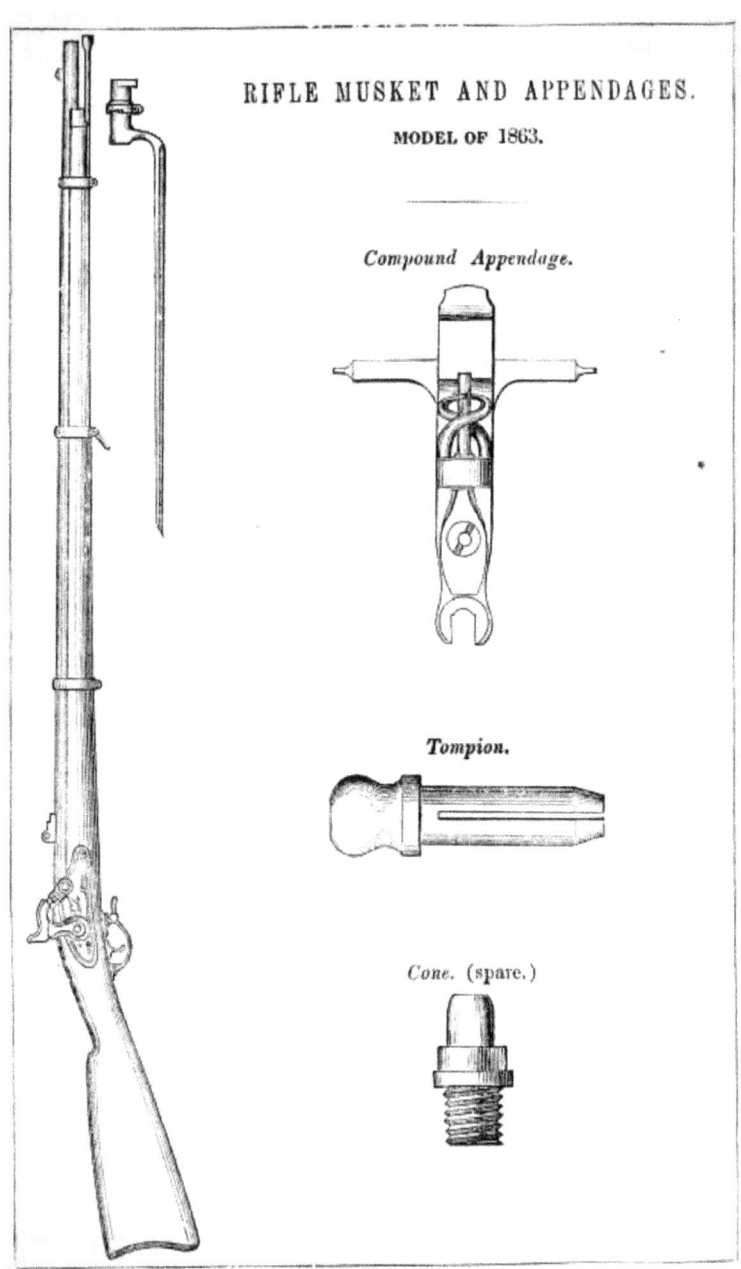

RIFLE MUSKET AND APPENDAGES.
MODEL OF 1863.

Compound Appendage.

Tompion.

Cone. (spare.)

MATERIALS OF WHICH THE PARTS ARE MADE.

Steel.

Tumbler; Lock-swivel; Feed-finger;
Finger-spring; Cover-catch; Sear;
Sear-spring; Mainspring;
Ramrod; Rear-sight, (except the screw;)
Screwdriver; Wiper; Ball-screw;
Cone; Tumbler and Wire Punch.

Malleable Iron.

Tip for Stock.

Wood.

Stock; Tompion.

Iron.

Socket of the Bayonet, and all other parts not enumerated.

Rules for Dismounting the Rifle Musket
Model of 1863.

1st. Unfix the bayonet (15.)
2nd. Put the tompion (45) into the muzzle of the barrel.
3rd. Draw the ramrod (5.)
4th. Turn out the tang-screw (3.)
5th. Take off the lock (16) to do this, first put the hammer at half-cock, then unscrew partially the side-screws (19 *a, b,*) and, with a slight tap on the head of each screw with a wooden instrument, loosen the lock from its bed in the stock, then turn out the side-screws and remove the lock with the left hand.

6th. Remove the side-screws (19 *a, b,*) taking care not to disturb the washers (41.)

7th. Take off the upper band (38) by first loosening the screw (*e.*)
8th. Take off the middle band (39) in the same manner.
9th. Take off the lower band (40) in the same manner.

Note.—The letter U on the bands is to indicate the upper side in assembling.

10th. Take out the barrel, (1.) In doing this, turn the musket horizontally, with the barrel downward, holding the barrel loosely with the left hand below the rear sight (6) the right hand grasping the stock by the handle; and if it does not leave the stock, tap the tompion in the muzzle gently against the ground or floor, which will loosen the breech end from the stock. This is preferable to lifting the barrel out by the muzzle, because if the tang of the breech-screw (2) should bind in the wood, the head of the stock (29 *d*) would be liable to be split by raising the muzzle first.

The foregoing parts are all that should usually be taken off or dismounted.

The soldier should never dismount the *guard, side-screw, washers, butt-plate, rear-sight,* and *cone,* except when an officer considers it necessary. The breech-screw should be taken out only by an armorer, and never in ordinary cleaning. The lock should not be taken apart, nor the bayonet clasp taken off, except when absolutely necessary in the opinion of an officer. *If proper and regular care be taken of the arm, this will be very seldom necessary.*

The musket being thus taken to pieces, proceed —

To Clean the Barrel.

1st. Stop the hole in the cone (4, *e*) with a peg of soft wood; pour a gill of water (warm if it can be had) into the muzzle; let it stand a short time to soften the deposit of the powder; put a plug of soft wood into the muzzle and shake the water up and down the barrel well; pour this out and repeat the washing until the water comes out clear; take out the peg from the cone and stand the barrel, muzzle downwards, to drain for a few moments.

2nd. Screw the wiper (44, *j*) on to the end of the ramrod (5, *d*) and put a piece of *dry cloth* or *tow* round it, sufficient to prevent it from chafing the grooves of the barrel; wipe the barrel quite dry, changing or drying the cloth two or three times.

3rd. Put no oil into the vent (4, *e*,) as it will clog the passage, and cause the cap to miss fire; but, with a slightly oiled rag on the wiper, rub the bore of the barrel and the face of the breech-screw (2, *e*,) and immediately insert the tompion (45) into the muzzle.

4th. To clean the exterior of the barrel, lay it flat on a bench or board, to avoid bending it. The practice of supporting the barrel at each end and rubbing it with a strap or buff-stick, or with the ramrod, or any other instrument, to *burnish* it, is pernicious, and should be strictly forbidden.

5th. After firing, the barrel should always be washed as soon as practicable; when the water comes off clear, wipe the barrel dry and pass into it a rag moistened with oil.

Fine *flour of emery* cloth is the best article to clean the exterior of the barrel.

To Clean the Lock.

Wipe every part with a moist rag and then a dry one; if any part of the interior shows rust, put a drop of oil on the point or end of a piece of soft wood dipped into *flour of emery*; rub out the rust clean and wipe the surface dry, then rub every part with a slightly oiled rag.

To Clean The Mountings.

For the mountings, and all of the iron and steel parts, use fine flour of emery moistened with oil, or flour of emery cloth.

For brass, use rotten-stone moistened with vinegar or water, and keep free from oil or grease. Use a hard brush, or a piece of soft pine, cedar, or crocus cloth.

Remove dirt from the screw holes by screwing a piece of soft wood into them.

Wipe clean with a linen rag and leave the parts slightly oiled.

In cleaning the arms great care should be observed *to preserve the qualities essential to service* rather than to obtain a bright polish.

Burnishing the barrel (or other parts) should be strictly avoided, as it tends to crook the barrel, and also to destroy the uniformity of the exterior finish of the arm.

It is not essential for the musket to be dismounted every time that it is cleaned, for after firing it in fine weather, or when there has been no chance for the wet to get between the barrel and the stock, it can be perfectly cleaned in the following manner:

Put a piece of rag or soft leather on the top of the cone and let the hammer down upon it; pour a gill of water into the muzzle carefully, so that it does not run down the outside; put a plug of wood into the muzzle and shake the gun up and down, changing the water repeatedly until it comes out clear. When clear, withdraw the leather and stand the musket on the muzzle a few moments, then wipe out the barrel, (as given in the second rule for cleaning,) and also wipe the exterior of the lock and the outside of the barrel around the cone and coneseat, first with a damp rag and then with a dry one, and lastly with a rag that has been slightly oiled. In this way all the dirt due to the firing may be removed without taking out a screw. If, however, the hammer is observed to work stiff, or to grate upon the tumbler, the lock must immediately be taken off and the parts cleaned and touched with oil.

To Reassemble the Musket.

The parts of the musket are put together in the inverse order of taking them apart, *viz*:

1st. The barrel. Drop the barrel into its place in the stock and squeeze it down with the hand; give the butt of the stock a gentle tap against the floor to settle the breech end of the barrel against the head of the stock (29, *d.*)

2nd. Put on the lower band with the letter U upward, being careful to loosen the screw so as not to mar the stock or barrel in sliding it into its place; screw it on firmly.

3rd. Put on the middle, and...

4th. The upper band in the same manner.

5th. The lock. 1st, half cock the hammer; take the lock in the right hand, with the main spring and sear toward you, holding the stock with the left hand by the swell, with the butt between the knees. Enter the lock fairly into the lock bed, taking care to keep the arm of the sear clear of the trigger; press the plate well down into the wood, and then turn the musket over, holding the lock and stock together with the left hand.

6th. With the right hand turn in the side screws, after having touched their screw-threads with oil. Observe that the point of the *rear* screw is *flat*, and should not project beyond the plate, to interfere with the hammer. The front screw has a round point.

7th. Turn in the tang-screw, after having oiled the screw-thread. Be careful to see that each of these screws are turned firmly home, *but not forced.*

Observe that the lock plays freely, without friction, and that no limb is bound by the wood.

8th. Return the ramrod.

9th. Refix the bayonet, after having oiled the clasp and socket, to prevent chafing.

10th. Replace the tompion. Oil the stock well with sperm or linseed oil; let it stand a few hours, then rub it with a woollen rag until the wood is perfectly dry. Repeat this from time to time, and it will produce a polish which moisture will not affect. Linseed oil is the best for this purpose, and it should be used while the arm is dismounted.

Rules for the More Complete Dismounting of the Rifle Musket When Cleaned by an Armourer

1st. The parts which are specially assigned to be dismounted by an experienced armourer will be stated in their regular order following No. 10, *viz*:

11th. Unscrew the cone, keeping the wrench well down on the square of the cone, to prevent the corners from being injured.

12th. Take out the guard-screws, (37.) *Note.*—The guard, butt-plate, and side-screw heads have conclave slits for which the screwdriver is adapted. This lessens the danger of the stock being marred by accident or carelessness in letting the screwdriver slip out while in the act of turning the screw. Great care should be taken to prevent injury in this particular.

13th. Take out the guard, using care to prevent injuring the wood at each end of the guard-plate, (33.)

14th. Take out the side-screw washers (41) with a drift-punch.

15th. Take out the butt-plate screws (31) with the largest blade of the screwdriver, (43 a,) and remove the butt-plate, (30.)

16th. Remove the rear-sight (6) by turning out the screw, (12,) which will release the sight from the barrel.

17th. Turn out the breech-screw, (2,) by means of a "*breech-screw wrench*" suited to the tenon (*b*) of the breech-screw. No other wrench should ever be used for this purpose, and the barrel should be held in the clamps fitting neatly the breech, (1 *a*.)

In reassembling the parts, the armorer is to observe the inverse order of taking them apart, *viz*:

1st. Breech-screw to be screwed into the barrel after being oiled;

2nd. Rear-sight to be affixed;
3rd. Butt-plate and screws;
4th. Side-screw washers;
5th. Guard;
6th. Guard-screws;
7th. The cone.

The remaining parts follow as given for the soldier, commencing with the barrel.

Order in Which the Lock is Taken Apart.

1st. Cock the piece, and apply the vise of the compound screw-driver (43 *b, c*) on the mainspring, let the hammer down to liberate the spring from the swivel (20) and mainspring-notch (18 *c.*) Remove the spring.

2nd. The sear-spring screw. Before turning this screw entirely out, strike the elbow of the spring with the screwdriver, so as to disengage the pivot from its mortise; then remove the screw and spring;

3rd. The sear-screw and sear;

4th. The bridle-screw and bridle;

5th. The tumbler-screw;

6th. The tumbler. This is driven out with a punch (44 *f*) inserted in the screw-hole, which at the same time liberates the hammer;

7th. Detach the mainspring swivel (20) from the tumbler with a drift-punch.

The lock is reassembled in the inverse order of taking apart, *viz*:

1st. The mainspring swivel;
2nd. Tumbler and hammer;
3rd. Tumbler-screw;
4th. Bridle and screw;
5th. Sear and screw;
6th. Sear-spring and screw;
7th. Mainspring.

Before replacing the screws oil them slightly with good sperm oil, putting a drop on the point of the screw; also on the arbour and pivot of the tumbler; between the movable branches of the springs and the lock-plate; on the hook and notches of the tumbler.

After the lock is put together, avoid turning the screws so hard as to make the limbs bind. To insure this, try the motion of each limb before and after its spring is mounted, and see that it moves without friction.

When a lock has from any cause become gummed with oil and dirt, it may be cleaned by being boiled in soap-suds, or in pearlash or soda-water, to loosen the thick oil; but heat should never be applied to any part of it in any other way.

As rust and dirt are produced by exploding caps or primers, although no charge be fired, the parts of the barrel and cone exposed should be carefully wiped and oiled after such practice.

Besides all the precautions in dismounting, remounting, and cleaning, which have been pointed out in the foregoing pages, habitual care in handling the arms is necessary to keep them in good and serviceable condition.

In *ordering arms* on parade, let the butt be brought gently to the ground, especially when the exercises take place on pavements or hard roads. This will save the mechanism of the lock from shocks, which are very injurious to it, and which tend to loosen and mar the screws and split the stock.

Rifled arms should not have the *ramrod sprung* in the bore with unnecessary force. It batters the head of the rod and wears injuriously the grooves. The soldier should let the rod slide down gently, supported by the thumb and finger; and the inspecting officer can satisfy himself of the condition of the bottom of the bore by gently tapping with the rod.

The face of the breech can be polished, after washing, by means of a cork fixed on the wiper or ball-screw; the polished surface can be seen if the muzzle is turned to the light.

In *stacking arms* care should be taken not to injure the bayonets by forcibly straining the edges against each other. The stack can be as well secured without such force being used.

No cutting, marking, or scraping, in any way, the wood or iron should be allowed; and no part of the gun should be touched with a file. Take every possible care to prevent water from getting in between the lock, or barrel, and stock. If any should get there, dismount the gun as soon as possible, clean and oil the parts as directed, and see that they are perfectly dry before reassembling them.

Mr. Dingee's Directions for Reblacking Belts

Brush them with a hard brush to clean the surface; if they are very greasy, use a wire scratch-brush, then with a soft brush or sponge apply the following mixture, *viz*: one gallon of soft water, two pounds of extract of logwood, half a pound of broken nut galls, boiled until the logwood is dissolved; when cold, add half a pint of the pyrolignite of iron—made by dissolving iron filings in pyroligneous acid, as much as the acid will take up.

The dye thus prepared should be well stirred and then left to settle. When clear decant it from the sediment and keep well corked for use.

Dry the belts in the shade, then apply a little sperm or olive oil and rub well with a hard brush.

Should any bad spots appear, scratch up the surface with the wire brush and wet two or three times with a simple decoction of gallnuts, or shumac, and again apply the dye as above.

The addition of the logwood is not essential; and a solution of copperas may replace, but not so well, the acetate of iron.

The model of 1863 corresponds with the model of 1861, except in the following particulars, *viz*:

Barrel.—The cone-seat is reduced in length about two tenths of an inch, fixing the centre of the cone, or vent, on a line with the face of the barrel, and dispensing with the cone-seat screw. The end of the muzzle is rounded to prevent being bruised.

Hammer.—The form of the hammer is changed to conform to that of the barrel, and otherwise improved.

Ramrod.—The "swell" is omitted and the body made larger, with a ball-screw cut on the small end, and a brass cap to protect it from injury.

Ramrod-spring.—Adopted instead of the swell to hold the rod in its place.

Bands.—Open bands fastened by screws instead of tight bands.

Band-springs.—Dispensed with as unnecessary.

Lock.—The lock is case-hardened in colours; the bands, swivels, and guard are blued in the same manner as the rear sight instead of being left bright.

Appendages.—The compound appendage for taking the arm apart is adopted in place of the spring-vise, ball-screw, tumbler, and band-spring punch of model 1861.

> Note.—The rules for dismounting and reassembling the rifle musket, model 1855, will apply to the model of 1863 by omitting the band-springs and the parts of the lock that apply to the "Maynard primer."

Infantry Tactics, for the Instruction,
Exercise, and Manoeuvres of the Soldier

Contents

Article 1   103
Article 2   108
School of the Soldier   112

INFANTRY TACTICS: TITLE 1

Article 1

FORMATION OF INFANTRY IN ORDER OF BATTLE.

1. In the formations of Infantry, a *Brigade of the line* will constitute the unit, and in every *line of battle* composed of more than one of these brigades, they will be posted from right to left, in the order of their numbers.

2. A similar disposition will be made of the regiments in a brigade.

3. In all exercises, manoeuvres, and evolutions, every regiment of ten companies will take the denomination of *battalion*, and all the battalions in the same *brigade* will be designated, from right to left, *first* battalion, *second* battalion, &c., &c. By these designations they will be known in the evolutions.

4. The interval between every two contiguous battalions in the same brigade will be *twenty-two* paces, and the interval between every two contiguous brigades will habitually be *one hundred and fifty* paces.

5. A less number of battalions than *four* will habitually be formed in one line of battle, but when it is thought expedient to form the brigade in two lines, the third and fourth battalions will be respectively posted in rear of the first and second battalions. The battalions of the first line will either be deployed, or in column at half distance, or closed in mass. The battalions of the second line will always be drawn up in column, either simple or double, at half distance or closed in mass, and posted for tactical instruction, one hundred and fifty paces in rear of the first line, counting from the front rank of the first, to the front rank of the second line. The battalions of the second line will be posted so that a line passing through their colours and those of the battalions of the first line respectively (whether deployed or in column) shall always be perpendicular to the line of battle. In presence of the enemy the distance between the lines will depend upon cir-

cumstances; in general, the second line should not be much exposed to the enemy's fire.

6. A regiment is composed of ten companies, which will be habitually posted from right to left in the following order: *First, sixth, fourth, ninth, third, eighth, fifth, tenth, seventh, second,* according to the rank of the captains.

7. With a less number of battalion companies, the same principle will be observed, *viz.*; the first captain will command the right company, the second captain the left company, the third captain the right centre company, and so on.

8. The companies thus posted will be designated from right to left, *first company, second company, &c.* This designation will he observed in the manoeuvres.

0-9. The other two companies, to be designated from time to time by the colonel, will be called the *companies of skirmishers.* The first company will habitually be posted thirty paces in rear of the file closers of the first, and the second thirty paces in rear of the file closers of the last battalion company.

0-10. Should the number of the regimental companies present, other than the companies of skirmishers, be less than eight, but one will be designated as skirmishers, to be in rear of the first or last battalion company, or divided into platoons, the first platoon in rear of the first, and the second in rear of the last battalion company, as the colonel may direct.

11. The first two battalion companies on the right, whatever their denomination, will form the first division; the next two companies the second division, and so on to the left.

12. Each company will be divided into two equal parts, which will be designated as the first and second platoon, counting from the right; and each platoon, in like manner, will be subdivided into two sections.

13. In all exercises and manoeuvres, every regiment, or part of a regiment, composed of two or more companies, will be designated as a battalion.

14, The colour, with a guard to be hereinafter designated, will be posted on the left of the right centre battalion company. That company, and all on its right, will be denominated the *right wing* of the battalion; the remaining companies the *left wing.*

15. The formation of a regiment is in two ranks; and each company will be formed into two ranks, in the following manner: the corporals will be posted in the front rank, and on the right and left of platoons,

according to height; the tallest corporal and the tallest man will form the first file, the next two tallest men will form the second file, and so on to the last file, which will be composed of the shortest corporal and the shortest man.

16. The odd and even files, numbered as one, two, in the company, from right to left, will form groups of four men, who will be designated *comrades in battle.*

17. The distance from one rank to another will be thirteen inches, measured from the breasts of the rear rank men to the backs or knapsacks of the front rank men.

18. For manoeuvring, the companies of a battalion will always be equalized, by transferring men from the strongest to the weakest companies.

Posts of Company Officers, Sergeants and Corporals.

19. The company officers and sergeants are nine in number, and will be posted in the following manner:

20. The *captain* on the right of the company, touching with the left elbow.

21. The *first sergeant* in the rear rank, touching with the left elbow, and covering the captain. In the manoeuvres he will be denominated *covering sergeant,* or *right guide* of the company.

22. The remaining officers and sergeants will be posted as file closers, and two paces behind the rear rank.

23. The *first lieutenant,* opposite the centre of the fourth section.

24. The *second lieutenant,* opposite the centre of the first platoon.

25. The *third lieutenant,* opposite the centre of the second platoon.

26. The *second sergeant,* opposite the second file from the left of the company. In the manoeuvres he will be designated *left guide* of the company.

27. The *third sergeant,* opposite the second file from the right of the second platoon.

28. The *fourth sergeant,* opposite the second file from the left of the first platoon.

29. The *fifth sergeant,* opposite the second file from the right of the first platoon.

30. In the left, or eighth company of the battalion, the second sergeant will be posted in the front rank, and on the left of the battalion.

31. The corporals will be posted in the front rank as prescribed, No. 15.

32. Absent officers and sergeants will be replaced—officers by sergeants, and sergeants by corporals. The colonel may detach a first lieutenant from one company to command another, of which both the captain and first lieutenant are absent; but this authority will give no right to a lieutenant to demand to be so detached.

Posts of Field Officers and Regimental Staff.

33. The field officers, colonel, lieutenant colonel and majors, are supposed to be mounted, and on active service shall be on horseback. The adjutant, when the battalion is manoeuvring, will be on foot.

34. The colonel will take post thirty-five paces in rear of the file closers, and opposite the centre of the battalion.

35. The lieutenant colonel and the senior major will be opposite the centres of the right and left wings respectively, and twelve paces in rear of the file closers. The junior major will take post thirty paces in rear of the file closers, and five paces to the right of the centre of the battalion; and he will, under the direction of the colonel, have the command of the companies of skirmishers.

36. The adjutant and sergeant major will be opposite the right and left of the battalion respectively, and eight paces in rear of the file closers.

37. The adjutant and sergeant major will aid the lieutenant colonel and senior major, respectively, in the manoeuvres.

38. The colonel, if absent, will be replaced by the lieutenant colonel, and the latter by one of the majors. If all the field officers be absent, the senior captain will command the battalion; but if either be present, he will not call the senior captain to act as field officer, except in case of evident necessity.

39. The quarter-master, surgeon and other staff officers, in one rank, on the left of the colonel, and three paces in his rear.

40. The quarter-master sergeant, the commissary sergeant, and the hospital steward on a line with the front rank of the field music, and two paces on the right.

Posts of Field Music and Band.

41. The buglers or musicians of the battalion companies will be drawn up in four ranks, and posted twelve paces in rear of the file closers, the left opposite the centre of the left centre company. The senior principal musician will be two paces in front of the field music, and the other two paces in the rear. In the companies of skirmishers,

the buglers will be in one rank, in a line with the front rank of the company, and four paces from its right flank.

42. The regimental band, if there be one, will be drawn up in two or four ranks, according to its numbers, and posted five paces in rear of the field music, having one of the principal musicians at its head.

Colour-Guard.

43. In each battalion the colour-guard will be composed of eight corporals, and posted on the left of the right-centre company, of which company, for the time being, the guard will make a part.

44. The front rank will be composed of a sergeant, to be selected by the colonel, who will be called, for the time, *colour-bearer*, with the two ranking corporals, respectively, on his right and left; the rear rank will be composed of the three corporals next in rank; and the three remaining corporals will be posted in their rear, and on the line of file closers. The left guide of the colour-company, when these three last named corporals are in the rank of file closers, will be immediately on their left.

45. In battalions with less than five companies present, there will be no colour-guard, and no display of colours, except it may be at reviews.

46. The corporals for the colour-guard will be selected from those most distinguished for regularity and precision, as well in their positions under arms as in their marching. The latter advantage, and a just carriage of the person, are to be more particularly sought for in the selection of the colour-bearer.

General Guides.

47. There will be two *general* guides in each battalion, selected, for the time, by the colonel, from among the sergeants (other than first sergeants) the most distinguished for carriage under arms, and accuracy in marching.

48. These sergeants will be respectively denominated, in the manoeuvres, *right general guide,* and *left general guide,* and be posted in the line of file closers; the first in rear of the right, and the second in rear of the left flank of the battalion.

Article 2

Instruction of the Battalion.

49. Every commanding officer is responsible for the instruction of his command. He will assemble the officers together for theoretical and practical instruction as often as he may judge necessary, and when unable to attend to this duty in person, it will be discharged by the officer next in rank.

50. Captains will be held responsible for the theoretical and practical instruction of their non-commissioned officers, and the adjutant for the instruction of the non-commissioned staff. To this end, they will require these tactics to be studied and recited, lesson by lesson; and when instruction is given on the ground, each non-commissioned officer, as he explains a movement, should be required to put it into practical operation.

51. The non-commissioned officers should also be practised in giving commands. Each command, in a lesson, at the theoretical instruction, should first be given by the instructor, and then repeated, in succession, by the non-commissioned officers, so that while they become habituated to the commands, uniformity may be established in the manner of giving them.

52. In the school of the soldier, the company officers will be the instructors of the squads; but if there be not a sufficient number of company officers present, intelligent sergeants may be substituted; and two or three squads, under sergeant instructors, be superintended, at the same time, by an officer.

53. In the school of the company, the lieutenant colonel and the majors, under the colonel, will be the principal instructors, substituting frequently the captain of the company, and sometimes one of the lieutenants; the substitute, as far as practicable, being superintended by one of the principals.

54. In the school of the battalion, the brigadier general may constitute himself the principal instructor, frequently substituting the colonel of the battalion, sometimes the lieutenant, colonel, or one of the majors, and twice or thrice, in the same course of instruction, each of the three senior captains. In this school, also, the substitute will always, if practicable, be superintended by the brigadier general or the colonel, or (in case of a captain being the instructor), by the lieutenant colonel or one of the majors.

55. Individual instruction being the basis of the instruction of companies, on which that of the regiment depends, and the first principles having the greatest influence upon this individual instruction, classes of recruits should be watched with the greatest care.

56. Instructors will explain, in a few clear and precise words, the movement to be executed; and not to overburden the memory of the men, they will always use the same terms to explain the same principles.

57. They should often join example to precept, should keep up the attention of the men by an animated tone, and pass rapidly from one movement to another, as soon as that which they command has been executed in a satisfactory manner.

58. The bayonet should only be fixed when required to be used, either for attack or defence; the exercises and manoeuvres will be executed without the bayonet.

59. In the movements which require the bayonet to be fixed, the chief of the battalion will cause the signal to *fix bayonet*, to be sounded; at this signal the men fix bayonets without command, and immediately replace their pieces in the position they were in before the signal.

INSTRUCTION OF OFFICERS.

60. The instruction of officers can be perfected only by joining theory to practice. The colonel will often practise them in marching and in estimating distances, and he will carefully endeavour to cause them to take steps equal in length and swiftness. They will also be exercised in the double quick step.

61. The instruction of officers will include all the Titles in this system of drill, as well as a perfect knowledge of the system of firing as prescribed by the War Department.

62. Every officer will make himself perfectly acquainted with the bugle signals; and should, by practice, be enabled, if necessary, to sound them. This knowledge, so necessary in general instruction, becomes of

vital importance on actual service in the field.

63. As the discipline and efficiency of a company materially depend on the conduct and character of its sergeants, they should be selected with care, and properly instructed in all the duties appertaining to their rank.

64. Their theoretical instruction should include the School of the Soldier, the School of the Company, and the Drill for Skirmishers; as also a knowledge of the principles of firing. They should likewise be well instructed in their duties as battalion guides.

65. The captain selects from the corporals in his company, those whom he judges fit to be admitted to the theoretical instruction of the sergeants.

Instruction of Corporals.

68. Their theoretical instruction should include the School of the Soldier, with a knowledge of firing.

67. The captain selects from his company a few privates, who may be admitted to the theoretical instruction of the corporals.

68. As the instruction of sergeants and corporals, is intended principally to qualify them for the instruction of the privates, they should be taught not only to execute, but to explain intelligibly everything they may be required to teach.

Commands.

There are three kinds.

69. The command of *caution*, which is *attention*.

70. The *preparatory command*, which indicates the movement which is to be executed.

71. The command of *execution*, such as *march* or *halt*, or, in the manual of arms, the part of command which causes an execution.

72. The tone of command should be animated, distinct, and of a loudness proportioned to the number of men under instruction.

73. The command *attention* is pronounced at the top of the voice, dwelling on the last syllable.

74. The command of *execution* will be pronounced in a tone firm and brief.

75. The commands of caution, and the preparatory commands, are herein distinguished by *italics*, those of execution by CAPITALS.

76. Those preparatory commands which, from their length, are difficult to be pronounced at once, must be divided into two or three

parts, with an ascending progression in the tone of command, but always in such a manner that the tone of execution may be more energetic and elevated; the divisions are indicated by a hyphen. The parts of commands which are placed in a parenthesis, are not pronounced.

INFANTRY TACTICS: TITLE 2

School of the Soldier

GENERAL RULES AND DIVISION OF THE SCHOOL OF THE SOLDIER.

77. The object of this school being the individual and progressive instruction of the recruits, the instructor never requires a movement to be executed until he has given an exact explanation of it; and he executes, himself, the movement which he commands, so as to join example to precept. He accustoms the recruit to take, by himself, the position which is explained—teaches him to rectify it only when required by his want of intelligence—and sees that all the movements are performed without precipitation.

78. Each movement should be understood before passing to another. After they have been properly executed in the order laid down in each lesson, the instructor no longer confines himself to that order; on the contrary, he should change it, that he may judge of the intelligence of the men.

79. The instructor allows the men to rest at the end of each part of the lessons, and oftener, if he thinks proper, especially at the commencement; for this purpose, he commands REST.

80. At the command REST, the soldier is no longer required to preserve immobility, or to remain in his place. If the instructor wishes merely to relieve the attention of the recruit, he commands, *in place—*REST; the soldier is then not required to preserve his immobility, but he always keeps one of his feet in its place.

81. When the instructor wishes to commence the instruction, he commands—ATTENTION; at the command, the soldier takes his position, remains motionless, and fixes his attention.

82. The *School of the Soldier* will be divided into three parts: the first, comprehending what ought to be taught to recruits without arms; the second, the manual of arms, the loadings and firings; the third, the principles of alignment, the march by the front, the different steps, the

march by the flank, the principles of wheeling, and those of change of direction; also, long marches in double quick time and the run.

83. Each part will be divided into lessons, as follows:

Part First.
Lesson 1. Position of the soldier without arms: Eyes right, left and front.
Lesson 2. Facings.
Lesson 3. Principles of the direct step in common and quick time.
Lesson 4. Principles of the direct step in double quick time and the run.

Part Second.
Lesson 1. Principles of shouldered arms.
Lesson 2. Manual of arms.
Lesson 3. To load in four times, and at will.
Lesson 4. Firings, direct, oblique, by file, and by rank.
Lesson 5. To fire and load, kneeling and lying.
Lesson 6. Bayonet exercise.

Part Third.
Lesson 1. Union of eight or twelve men for instruction in the principles of alignment.
Lesson 2. The direct march, the oblique march, and the different steps.
Lesson 3. The march by the flank.
Lesson 4. Principles of wheeling and change of direction.
Lesson 5. Long marches and double quick time, and the run, with arms and knapsacks.

Part First.

84. This will be taught, if practicable, to one recruit at a time; but three or four may be united, when the number is great, compared with that of the instructors. In this case, the recruits will be placed in a single rank, at one pace from each other. In this part, the recruits will be without arms.

Lesson 1: Position of a Soldier.

85. Heels on the same line, as near each other as the conformation of the man will permit;

The feet turned out equally, and forming with each other something less than a right angle;

The knees straight without stiffness;
The body erect on the hips, inclining a little forward;
The shoulders square and falling equally;
The arms hanging naturally;
The elbows near the body;
The palm of the hand turned a little to the front, the little finger behind the seam of the pantaloons;
The head erect and square to the front, without constraint;
The chin near the stock, without covering it;
The eyes fixed straight to the front, and striking the ground about the distance of fifteen paces.

Remarks on the Position of a Soldier.

Heels on the same line;

86. Because, if one were in rear of the other, the shoulder on that side would be thrown back, or the position of the soldier would be constrained.

Heels more or less closed

Because men who are knock-kneed, or who have legs with large calves, cannot, without constraint, make their heels touch while standing.

The feet equally turned out, and not forming too large an angle;

Because, if one foot were turned out more than the other, a shoulder would be deranged, and if both feet be too much turned out, it would not be practicable to incline the upper part of the body forward without rendering the whole position unsteady.

Knees extended without stiffness;

Because, if stiffened, constraint and fatigue would be unavoidable.

The body erect on the hips;

Because it gives equilibrium to the position. The instructor will observe that many recruits have the bad habit of dropping a shoulder, of drawing in a side, or of advancing a hip, particularly the right, when under arms. These are defects he will labour to correct.

The upper part of the body inclining forward;

Because commonly, recruits are disposed to do the reverse, to project the belly, and to throw back the shoulders, when they wish to hold themselves erect, from which result great inconveniences in marching. The habit of inclining forward the upper part of the body is so important to contract, that the instructor must enforce it at the beginning, particularly with recruits who have naturally the opposite habit.

Shoulders square;

Because, if the shoulders be advanced beyond the line of the breast, and the back arched (the defect called *round-shouldered*, not uncommon among recruits), the man cannot align himself, nor use his piece with address. It is important, then, to correct this defect, and necessary to that end that the coat should set easy about the shoulders and armpits; but in correcting this defect, the instructor will take care that the shoulders be not thrown too much to the rear, which would cause the belly to project, and the small of the back to be curved.

The arms hanging naturally, elbows near the body, the palm of the hand a little turned to the front, the little finger behind the seam of the pantaloons;

Because these positions are equally important to the *shoulder-arms*, and to prevent the man from occupying more space in a rank than is necessary to a free use of the piece; they have, moreover, the advantage of keeping in the shoulders.

The face straight to the front, and without constraint;

Because, if there be stiffness in the latter position, it would communicate itself to the whole of the upper part of the body, embarrass its movements, and give pain and fatigue.

Eyes direct to the front;

Because this is the surest means of maintaining the shoulders in line—an essential object, to be insisted on and attained.

87. The instructor having given the recruit the position of the soldier without arms, will now teach him the turning of the head and eyes. He will command:

1. *Eyes*—RIGHT. 2. FRONT.

88. At the word *right*, the recruit will turn the head gently, so as to bring the inner corner of the left eye in a line with the buttons of the coat, the eyes fixed on the line of the eyes of the men in, or supposed to be in, the same rank.

89. At the second command, the head will resume the direct or habitual position.

90. The movement of *Eyes*—LEFT will be executed by inverse means.

91. The instructor will take particular care that the movement of the head does not derange the squareness of the shoulders, which will

happen if the movement of the former be too sudden.

92. When the instructor shall wish the recruit to pass from the state of attention to that of ease, he will command:

REST.

93. To cause a resumption of the habitual position, the instructor will command:

1. *Attention.* 2. SQUAD.

94. At the first word, the recruit will fix his attention; at the second, he will resume the prescribed position and steadiness.

Lesson 2: Facings.

95. Facing to the right and left will be executed in one *time*, or pause. The instructor will command:

1. *Squad,* 2. *Right (or left)*—FACE.

96. At the second command, raise the right foot slightly, turn on the left heel, raising the toes a little, and then replace the right heel by the side of the left, and on the same line.

97. The full face to the rear (or front) will be executed in two *times*, or pauses. The instructor will command.

1. *Squad,* 2. ABOUT—FACE.

98. (*First time,*) At the word *about*, the recruit will turn on the left heel, bring the left toe to the front, carry the right foot to the rear, the hollow opposite to, and full three inches from, the left heel, the feet square to each other.

99. (*Second time.*) At the word *face*, the recruit will turn on both heels, raise the toes a little, extend the hams, face to the rear, bringing, at the same time, the right heel by the side of the left.

100. The instructor will take care that these motions do not derange the position of the body.

Lesson 3: Principles of the Direct Step.

101. The length of the direct step, or pace, in common time, will be twenty-eight inches, reckoning from heel to heel, and in swiftness, at the rate of ninety in a minute.

102. The instructor, seeing the recruit confirmed in his position, will explain to him the principle and mechanism of this step—placing himself six or seven paces from, and facing to, the recruit. He will himself execute slowly the step in the way of illustration, and then command:

1. *Squad, forward.* 2. *Common time,* 3. MARCH.

103. At the first command, the recruit will throw the weight of the body on the right leg, without bending the left knee.

104. At the third command, he will smartly, but without a jerk, carry straight forward the left foot twenty-eight inches from the right, the sole near the ground, the ham extended, the toe a little depressed, and, as also the knee, slightly turned out; he will, at the same time, throw the weight of the body forward, and plant flat the left foot, without shock, precisely at the distance where it finds itself from the right when the weight of the body is brought forward, the whole of which will now rest on the advanced foot. The recruit will next, in like manner, advance the right foot and plant it as above, the heel twenty-eight inches from the heel of the left foot, and thus continue to march without crossing the legs, or striking the one against the other, without turning the shoulders, and preserving always the face direct to the front.

105. When the instructor shall wish to arrest the march, he will command:

1. *Squad*, 2. HALT.

106. At the second command, which will be given at the instant when either foot is coming to the ground, the foot in the rear will be brought up, and planted by the side of the other, without shock.

107. The instructor will indicate, from time to time, to the recruit, the cadence of the step by giving the command *one* at the instant of raising a foot, and *two* at the instant it ought to be planted, observing the cadence of ninety steps in a minute. This method will contribute greatly to impress upon the mind the two motions into which the step is naturally divided.

108. Common time will be employed only in the first and second parts of the School for the Soldier. As soon as the recruit has acquired steadiness, has become established in the principles of shouldered arms, and in the mechanism, length and swiftness of the step in common time, he will be practised only in quick time, the double quick time, and the run.

109. The principles of the step in quick time are the same as for common time, but its swiftness is at the rate of one hundred and ten steps per minute.

110. The instructor wishing the squad to march in quick time, will command:

1. *Squad, forward.* 2. MARCH.

Lesson 4: Principles of the Double Quick Step.

111. The length of the double quick step is thirty-three inches, and its swiftness at the rate of one hundred and sixty-five steps per minute.

112. The instructor wishing to teach the recruits the principles and mechanism of the double quick step, will command:

1. *Double quick step.* 2. MARCH.

113. At the first command the recruit will raise his hands to a level with his hips, the hands closed, the nails toward the body, the elbows to the rear.

114. At the second command, he will raise to the front his left leg bent, in order to give to the knee the greatest elevation, the part of the leg between the knee and the instep vertical, the toe depressed; he will then replace his foot in its former position; with the right leg he will execute what has just been prescribed for the left, and the alternate movement of the legs will be continued until the command:

1. *Squad.* 2. HALT.

115. At the second command, the recruit will bring the foot which is raised by the side of the other, and dropping at the same time his hands by his side, will resume the position of the soldier without arms.

116. The instructor placing himself seven or eight paces from, and facing the recruit, will indicate the cadence by the commands *one* and *two*, given alternately at the instant each foot should be brought to the ground, which at first will be in common time, but its rapidity will be gradually augmented.

117. The recruit being sufficiently established in the principles of this step, the instructor will command:

1. *Squad, forward.* 2. *Double quick* 3. MARCH.

118. At the first command, the recruit will throw the weight of his body on the right leg.

119. At the second command he will place his arms as indicated No. 113.

120. At the third command, he will carry forward the left foot, the leg slightly bent, the knee somewhat raised—will plant his left foot, the toe first, thirty-three inches from the right, and with the right foot will then execute what has just been prescribed for the left. This alternate movement of the legs will take place by throwing the weight of the body on the foot that is planted, and by allowing a natural, oscillatory motion to the arms.

121. The double quick step may be executed with different degrees of swiftness. Under urgent circumstances the cadence of this

step may be increased to one hundred and eighty per minute. At this rate a distance of four thousand yards would be passed over in about twenty-five minutes.

122. The recruits will be exercised also in running.

123. The principles are the same as for the double quick step, the only difference consisting in a greater degree of swiftness.

124. It is recommended in marching at double quick time, or the run, that the men should breathe as much as possible through the nose, keeping the mouth closed. Experience has proved that, by conforming to this principle, a man can pass over a much longer distance, and with less fatigue.

Part Second

General Rules.

125. The instructor will not pass the men to this second part until they shall be well established in the position of the body, and in the manner of marching at the different steps.

126. He will then unite four men, whom he will place in the same rank, elbow to elbow, and instruct them in the position of shouldered arms, as follows:

Lesson 1: Principles of Shouldered Arms.

127. The recruit being placed as explained in the first lesson of the first part, the instructor will cause him to bend the right arm slightly, and place the piece in it, in the following manner:

128. The piece in the right hand—the barrel nearly vertical and resting in the hollow of the shoulder—the guard to the front, the arm hanging nearly at its full length near the body; the thumb and forefinger embracing the guard, the remaining fingers closed together, and grasping the swell of the stock just under the cock, which rests on the little finger.

129. Recruits are frequently seen with natural defects in the conformation of the shoulders, breast and hips. These the instructor will labour to correct in the lessons without arms, and afterwards, by steady endeavours, so that the appearance of the pieces, in the same line, may be uniform, and this without constraint to the men in their positions.

130. The instructor will have occasion to remark that recruits, on first bearing arms, are liable to derange their position by lowering the right shoulder and the right hand, or by sinking the hip and spreading out the elbows.

131. He will be careful to correct all these faults by continually rectifying the position; he will sometimes take away the piece to replace it the better; he will avoid fatiguing the recruits too much in the beginning, but labour by degrees to render this position so natural and easy that they may remain in it a long time without fatigue.

132. Finally, the instructor will take great care that the piece, at a shoulder, be not carried too high nor too low: if too high, the right elbow would spread out, the soldier would occupy too much space in his rank, and the piece be made to waver; if too low, the files would be too much closed, the soldier would not have the necessary space to handle his piece with facility, the right arm would become too much fatigued, and would draw down the shoulder.

133. The instructor, before passing to the second lesson, will cause to be Repeated the movements of *eyes right, left* and *front*, and the *facings*.

Lesson 2: Manual of Arms.

134. The manual of arms will be taught to four men, placed, at first, in one rank, elbow to elbow, and afterwards in two ranks.

135. Each command will be executed in one *time* (or pause), but this time will be divided into motions, the better to make known the mechanism.

136. The rate, (or swiftness) of each motion, in the manual of arms, with the exceptions herein indicated, is fixed at the ninetieth part of a minute; but, in order not to fatigue the attention, the instructor will, at first, look more particularly to the execution of the motions, without requiring a nice observance of the cadence, to which he will bring the recruits progressively, and after they shall have become a little familiarized with the handling of the piece.

137. As the motions relative to the cartridge, to the rammer, and to the fixing and unfixing of the bayonet, cannot be executed at the rate prescribed, nor even with a uniform swiftness, they will not be subjected to that cadence. The instructor will, however, labour to cause these motions to be executed with promptness, and, above all, with regularity.

138. The last syllable of the command will decide the brisk execution of the first motion of each time (or pause). The commands *two, three*, and *four*, will decide the brisk execution of the other motions. As soon as the recruits shall well comprehend the positions of the several motions of a time, they will be taught to execute the time without resting on its different motions; the mechanism of the time will nev-

Shouldered arms. N.º 127.

Support arms. N.º 139.

ertheless be observed, as well to give a perfect use of the piece, as to avoid the sinking of, or slurring over, either of the motions.

139. The manual of arms will be taught in the following progression; the instructor will command:

Support—ARMS.

One time and three motions,

140. (*First motion.*) Bring the piece, with the right hand, perpendicularly to the front and between the eyes, the barrel to the rear; seize the piece with the left hand at the lower band, raise this hand as high as the chin, and seize the piece at the same time with the right hand four inches below the cock.

141. (*Second motion.*) Turn the piece with the right hand, the barrel to the front; carry the piece to the left shoulder, and pass the fore-arm extended on the breast between the right hand and the cock; support the cock against the left fore-arm, the left hand resting on the right breast.

142. (*Third motion.*) Drop the right hand by the side.

143. When the instructor may wish to give repose in this position, he will command:

REST.

144. At this command, the recruits will bring up smartly the right hand to the handle of the piece (small of the stock), when they will not be required to preserve silence, or steadiness of position.

145. When the instructor may wish the recruits to pass from this position to that of silence and steadiness, he will command:

1. *Attention.* 2. SQUAD.

146. At the second word, the recruits will resume the position of the third motion of *support arms*.

Shoulder—ARMS.

One time and three motions.

147. (*First motion.*) Grasp the piece with the right hand under and against the left fore-arm; seize it with the left hand at the lower band, the thumb extended; detach the piece slightly from the shoulder, the left fore-arm along the stock.

148. (*Second motion.*) Carry the piece vertically to the right shoulder with both hands, the rammer to the front, change the position of the right hand so as to embrace the guard with the thumb and fore-finger, slip the left hand to the height of the shoulder, the fingers extended and joined, the right arm nearly straight.

149. (*Third motion.*) Drop the left hand quickly by the side.

Present arms. N.º 149.

Ordered arms. N.º 156.

Present—ARMS.

One time and two motions.

150. (*First motion.*) With the right hand bring the piece erect before the centre of the body, the rammer to the front; at the same time seize the piece with the left hand half-way between the guide sight and lower band, the thumb extended along the barrel and against the stock, the forearm horizontal and resting against the body, the hand as high as the elbow.

151. (*Second motion,*) Grasp the small of the stock with the right hand, below and against the guard.

Shoulder—ARMS.

One time and two motions,

152. (*First motion.*) Bring the piece to the right shoulder, at the same time change the position of the right hand so as to embrace the guard with the thumb and fore-finger, slip up the left hand to the height of the shoulder, the fingers extended and joined, the right arm nearly straight.

153. (*Second motion.*) Drop the left hand quickly by the side.

Order—ARMS.

One time and two motions.

154. (*First motion.*) Seize the piece briskly with the left hand near the upper band, and detach it slightly from the shoulder with the right hand: loosen the grasp of the right hand, lower the piece with the left, reseize the piece with the right hand above the lower band, the little finger in the rear of the barrel, the butt about four inches from the ground, the right hand supported against the hip, drop the left hand by the side. If the rifle musket is used, the piece will be seized by the left hand a little above the middle band, and it will be seized by the right hand, just above the lower band.

155. (*Second motion.*) Let the piece slip through the right hand to the ground by opening slightly the fingers, and take the position about to be described.

POSITION OF ORDER ARMS.

156. The hand low, the barrel between the thumb and fore-finger extended along the stock; the other fingers extended and joined; the muzzle about two inches from the right shoulder; the rammer in front; the toe (or beak) of the butt, against, and in a line with, the toe of the right foot, the barrel perpendicular.

157. When the instructor may wish to give repose in this position, he will command:

REST.

158. At this command, the recruits will not be required to preserve silence or steadiness.

159. When the instructor may wish the recruits to pass from this position to that of silence and steadiness, he will command:

1. *Attention*, 2. SQUAD.

160. At the second word, the recruits will resume the position of *order arms*.

Shoulder—ARMS.

One time and two motions.

161. (*First motion.*) Raise the piece vertically with the right hand to the height of the right breast, and opposite the shoulder, the elbow close to the body; seize the piece with the left hand below the right, and drop quickly the right hand to grasp the piece at the swell of the stock, the thumb and fore-finger embracing the guard; press the piece against the shoulder with the left hand, the right arm nearly straight.

162. (*Second motion,*) Drop the left hand quickly by the side.

LOAD IN NINE TIMES.

1. LOAD.

One time and one motion,

163. Grasp the piece with the left hand as high as the right elbow, and bring it vertically opposite the middle of the body, shift the right hand to the upper band, place the butt between the feet, the barrel to the front; seize it with the left hand near the muzzle, which should be three inches from the body; carry the right hand to the cartridge-box. If the rifle musket is used the right hand will be shifted to just below the upper band. The muzzle will be eight inches from the body.

2. *Handle*—CARTRIDGE.

One time and one motion.

164. Seize the cartridge with the thumb and next two fingers, and place it between the teeth.

3. *Tear*—CARTRIDGE.

One time and one motion,

165. Tear the paper to the powder, hold the cartridge upright between the thumb and first two fingers, near the top; in this position place it in front of and near the muzzle—the back of the hand to the front.

4. *Charge*—CARTRIDGE.

One time and one motion.

166. Empty the powder into the barrel: disengage the ball from the paper with the right hand and the thumb and first two fingers of the left; insert it into the bore, the pointed end uppermost, and press it down with the right thumb; seize the head of the rammer with the thumb and fore-finger of the right hand, the other fingers closed, the elbows near the body.

5. *Draw*—RAMMER.
One time and three motions.

167. (*First motion.*) Half draw the rammer by extending the right arm; steady it in this position with the left thumb; grasp the rammer near the muzzle with the right hand, the little finger uppermost, the nails to the front, the thumb extended along the rammer.

168. (*Second motion.*) Clear the rammer from the pipes by again extending the arm; the rammer in the prolongation of the pipes.

169. (*Third motion.*) Turn the rammer, the little end of the rammer passing near the left shoulder; place the head of the rammer on the ball, the back of the hand to the front.

6. *Ram*—CARTRIDGE.
One time and one motion.

170. Insert the rammer as far as the right, and steady it in this position with the thumb of the left hand; seize the rammer at the small end with the thumb and fore-finger of the right hand, the back of the hand to the front; press the ball home, the elbows near the body.

7. *Return*—RAMMER.
One time and three motions.

171. (*First motion.*) Draw the rammer halfway out, and steady it in this position with the left thumb; grasp it near the muzzle with the right hand, the little finger uppermost, the nails to the front, the thumb along the rammer: clear the rammer from the bore by extending the arm, the nails to the front, the rammer in the prolongation of the bore.

172. (*Second motion.*) Turn the rammer, the head of the rammer passing near the left shoulder, and insert it in the pipes until the right hand reaches the muzzle, the nails to the front.

173. (*Third motion.*) Force the rammer home by placing the little finger of the right hand on the head of the rammer; pass the left hand down the barrel to the extent of the arm, without depressing the shoulder.

8. PRIME.
One time and two motions.

Load. N.º 163.

Prime N.º 174.

174. (*First motion.*) With the left hand raise the piece till the hand is as high as the eye, grasp the small of the stock with the right hand; half face to the right; place, at the same time, the right foot behind and at right angles with the left; the hollow of the right foot against the left heel. Slip the left hand down to the lower band, the thumb along the stock, the left elbow against the body; bring the piece to the right side, the butt below the right fore-arm—the small of the stock against the body and two inches below the right breast, the barrel upwards, the muzzle on a level with the eye.

175. (*Second motion.*) Half cock with the thumb of the right hand, the fingers supported against the guard and the small of the stock—remove the old cap with one of the fingers of the right hand, and with the thumb and forefinger of the same hand, take a cap from the pouch, place it on the nipple, and press it down with the thumb; seize the small of the stock with the right hand.

9. Shoulder—ARMS.

One time and two motions,

176. (*First motion.*) Bring the piece to the right shoulder and support it there with the left hand, face to the front; bring the right heel to the side of and on a line with the left; grasp the piece with the right hand as indicated in the position of *shoulder arms.*

177. (*Second motion.*) Drop the left hand quickly by the side.

READY

One time and three motions.

178. (*First motion.*) Raise the piece slightly with the right hand, making a half face to the right on the left heel; carry the right foot to the rear, and place it at right angles to the left, the hollow of it opposite to and against the left heel; grasp the piece with the left hand at the lower band and detach it slightly from the shoulder.

179. (*Second motion.*) Bring down the piece with both hands, the barrel upward, the left thumb extended along the stock, the butt below the right fore-arm, the small of the stock against the body and two inches below the right breast, the muzzle as high as the eye, the left elbow against the side; place at the same time the right thumb on the head of the cock, the other fingers under and against the guard.

180. (*Third motion.*) Cock, and seize the piece at the small of the stock without deranging the position of the butt.

AIM.

One time and one motion.

181. Raise the piece with both hands, and support the butt against

the right shoulder; the left elbow down, the right as high as the shoulder; incline the head upon the butt, so that the right eye may perceive quickly the notch of the hausse, the front sight, and the object aimed at, the left eye closed, the right thumb extended along the stock, the fore-finger on the trigger.

182. When recruits are formed in two ranks to execute the firings, the front rank men will raise a little less the right elbow, in order to facilitate the aim of the rear rank men.

183. The rear rank men, in aiming, will each carry the right foot about eight inches to the right, and towards the left heel of the man next on the right, inclining the upper part of the body forward.

FIRE.
One time and one motion,

184. Press the fore-finger against the trigger, fire, without lowering or turning the head, and remain in this position.

185. Instructors will be careful to observe when the men fire, that they aim at some distinct object, and that the barrel be so directed that the line of fire and the line of sight be in the same vertical plane. They will often cause the firing to be executed on ground of different inclinations, in order to accustom the men to fire at objects either above or below them.

LOAD.
One time and one motion.

186. Bring down the piece with both hands, at the same time face to the front and take the position of *load* as indicated, No. 163. Each rear rank man will bring his right foot by the side of the left.

187. The men being in this position, the instructor will cause the loading to be continued by the commands and means prescribed, No. 163, and following.

188. If, after firing, the instructor should not wish the recruits to reload, he will command:

Shoulder—ARMS.
One time and one motion

189. Throw up the piece briskly with the left hand and resume the position of *shoulder arms*, at the same time face to the front, turning on the left heel, and bring the right heel on a line with the left.

190. To accustom the recruits to wait for the command *fire*, the instructor, when they are in the position of *aim*, will command:

Recover—ARMS.
One time and one motion.

Aim—No. 181.

When deployed as skirmisher, to aim with rear sight at high elevation.

191. At the first part of the command, withdraw the finger from the trigger; at the command *arms*, retake the position of the third motion of *ready*.

192. The recruits being in the position of the third motion of *ready*, if the instructor should wish to bring them to a shoulder, he will command:

Shoulder—ARMS.

One time and one motion.

193. At the command *shoulder*, place the thumb upon the cock, the fore-finger on the trigger, half cock, and seize the small of the stock with the right hand. At the command *arms*, bring up the piece briskly to the right shoulder, and retake the position of shoulder arms.

REMARKS ON LOADING AND FIRING.

194. Whenever the loadings and firings are to be executed, and the cartridge-boxes are slung upon the waist-belt, the instructor will cause them to be brought to the front.

195. If Maynard's primer be used the command will be

Load in eight times.

and the eighth command will be *shoulder arms*, and executed from *return rammer* in one time and two motions, as follows:

(*First motion.*) Raise the piece with the left hand, and take the position of shoulder arms as indicated No. 152.

(*Second motion.*) Drop the left hand quickly by the side.

196. The recruits being at shoulder arms, when the instructor shall wish to fix bayonets, he will command:

Fix—BAYONET.

One time and three motions,

197. (*First motion.*) Grasp the piece with the left hand at the height of the shoulder, and detach it slightly from the shoulder with the right hand.

198. (*Second motion.*) Quit the piece with the right hand, lower it with the left hand, opposite the middle of the body, and place the butt between the feet without shock; the rammer to the rear, the barrel vertical, the muzzle three inches from the body; seize it with the right hand at the upper band, and carry the left hand reversed to the handle of the bayonet. If the rifle musket be used the barrel will be inclined forward, the muzzle eight inches from the body, and the left hand reversed to the handle of the bayonet.

199. (*Third motion.*) Draw the bayonet from the scabbard and fix it

on the extremity of the barrel; seize the piece with the left hand, the arm extended, the right hand at the upper band. If the rifle musket be used the clasp will be turned as soon as the bayonet is fixed upon the barrel.

Shoulder—ARMS.

One time and two motions,

200. (*First motion.*) Raise the piece with the left hand and place it against the right shoulder, the rammer to the front: seize the piece at the same time with the right hand at the swell of the stock, the thumb and fore-finger embracing the guard, the right arm nearly extended,

201. (*Second motion.*) Drop briskly the left hand by the side.

Charge—BAYONET.

One time and two motions,

202. (First motion,) Raise the piece slightly with the right hand and make a half face to the right on the left heel; place the hollow of the right foot opposite to, and three inches from the left heel, the feet square; seize the piece at the same time with the left hand a little above the lower band.

203. (*Second motion.*) Bring down the piece with both hands, the barrel uppermost, the left elbow against the body; seize the small of the stock, at the same time, with the right hand, which will be supported against the hip; the point of the bayonet as high as the ere.

Shoulder—ARMS.

One time and two motions,

204. (*First motion.*) Throw up the piece briskly with the left hand in facing to the front, place it against the right shoulder, the rammer to the front; turn the right hand so as to embrace the guard, slide the left hand to the height of the shoulder, the right hand nearly extended.

205. (*Second motion.*) Drop the left hand smartly by the side.

Trail—ARMS.

One time and two motions,

206. (*First motion.*) The same as the first motion of order arms.

207. (*Second motion.*) Incline the muzzle slightly to the front, the butt to the rear and about four inches from the ground. The right hand supported at the hip, will so hold the piece that the rear rank men may not touch with their bayonets the men in the front rank.

Shoulder—ARMS.

208. At the command *shoulder*, raise the piece perpendicularly in the right hand, the little finger in the rear of the barrel; at the command *arms*, execute what has been prescribed for the *shoulder* from the

Charge bayonet.—No. 202.

Unfix bayonet.—No. 209.

position of *order arms*.

Unfix—BAYONET.
One time and three motions.

209. (*First and second motions.*) The same as the first and second motions of *fix bayonet,* except that, at the end of the second command, the thumb of the right hand will be placed on the spring of the sabre-bayonet, and the left hand will embrace the handle of the sabre-bayonet and the barrel, the thumb extended along the blade. If the rifle musket is used, at the end of the second command turn the clasp of the bayonet by pressing against it with the thumb of the left hand, and then grasp the socket of the bayonet with the left hand, the shank resting between the thumb and fore-finger, the thumb pointed up.

210. (*Third motion.*) Press the thumb of the right hand on the spring, wrest off the sabre-bayonet, turn it to the right, the edge to the front, lower the guard until it touches the right hand, which will seize the back and the edge of the blade between the thumb and first two fingers, the other fingers holding the piece; change the position of the hand without quitting the handle, return the sabre-bayonet to the scabbard, and seize the piece with the left hand, the arm extended. If the rifle musket is used, the following will be the method, *viz*.: (*Third motion.*) Wrest off the bayonet, turn it to the right, bringing the point of the bayonet down; change the position of the hand without quitting hold of the shank of the socket, return the bayonet to the scabbard, and seize the piece with the left hand, the arm extended.

Shoulder—ARMS.
One time and two motions,

211. (*First motion.*) The same as the first motion from *fix bayonet,* No. 200.

212. (*Second motion.*) The same as the second motion from fix 'bayonet., No. 201.

Secure—ARMS.
One time and three motions,

213. (*First motion.*) The same as the first motion of *support arms,* No. 140, except with the right hand seize the piece at the small of the stock.

214. (*Second motion.*) Turn the piece with both hands, the barrel to the front; bring it opposite the left shoulder, the butt against the hip, the left hand at the lower band, the thumb as high as the chin and extended on the rammer; the piece erect and detached from the shoulder, the left fore-arm against the piece.

Secure Arms.—No. 213.

Right shoulder shift arms.—No. 219.

215. (*Third motion.*) Reverse the piece, pass it under the left arm, the left hand remaining at the lower band, the thumb on the rammer to prevent it from sliding out, the little finger resting against the hip, the right hand falling at the same time by the side.

Shoulder—ARMS.

One time and three motions.

216. (*First motion.*) Raise the piece with the left hand, and seize it with the right hand at the small of the stock. The piece erect and detached from the shoulder, the butt against the hip, the left fore-arm along the piece.

217. (*Second motion.*) The same as the second motion of *shoulder arms from a support.*

218. (*Third motion.*) The same as the third motion of shoulder arms from a support.

Right shoulder shift—ARMS.

One time and two motions.

219. (*First motion.*) Detach the piece perpendicularly from the shoulder with the right hand, and seize it with the left between the lower band and guide-sight, raise the piece, the left hand at the height of the shoulder and four inches from it; place, at the same time, the right hand on the butt, the beak between the first two fingers, the other two fingers under the butt plate.

220. (*Second motion.*) Quit the piece with the left hand, raise and place the piece on the right shoulder with the right hand, the lock plate upward; let fall at the same time, the left hand by the side.

Shoulder—ARMS.

One time and two motions.

221. (*First motion.*) Raise the piece perpendicularly by extending the right arm to its full length, the rammer to the front; at the same time seize the piece with the left hand between the lower band and guide sight.

222. (*Second motion.*) Quit the butt with the right hand, which will immediately embrace the guard, lower the piece to the position of shoulder arms, slide up the left hand to the height of the shoulder, the fingers extended and closed. Drop the left hand by the side.

223. The men being at support arms, the instructor will sometimes cause pieces to be brought to the right shoulder. To this effect he will command:

Right shoulder shift—ARMS.

One time and two motions.

224. (*First motion.*) Seize the piece with the right hand, below and near the left fore-arm, place the left hand under the butt, the heel of the butt between the first two fingers.

225. (*Second motion.*) Turn the piece with the left hand, the lock plate upward, carry it to the right shoulder, the left hand still holding the butt, the muzzle elevated; hold the piece in this position and place the right hand upon the butt, as is prescribed No. 219, and let fall the left hand by the side.

Support—ARMS.

One time and two motions.

226. (*First motion.*) The same as the first motion of *shoulder arms*, No. 221.

227. (*Second motion*) Turn the piece with both hands, the barrel to the front, carry it opposite the left shoulder, slip the right hand to the small of the stock, place the left fore-arm extended on the breast, as is prescribed No. 141, and let fall the right hand by the side.

Arms—AT WILL.

One time and one motion,

228. At this command, carry the piece at pleasure on either shoulder, with one or both hands, the muzzle elevated.

Shoulder—ARMS.

One time and one motion.

229. At this command, retake quickly the position of shoulder arms.

230. The recruits being at ordered arms, when the instructor shall wish to cause the pieces to be placed on the ground, he will command:

Ground—ARMS.

One time and two motions,

231. (First motion.) Turn the piece with the right hand, the barrel to the left, at the same time seize the cartridge box with the left hand, bend the body, advance the left foot, the heel opposite the lower band; lay the piece on the ground with the right hand, the toe of the butt on a line with the right toe, the knees slightly bent, the right heel raised.

232. (*Second motion,*) Rise up, bring the left foot by the side of the right, quit the cartridge box with the left hand, and drop the hands by the side.

Raise—ARMS.

One time and two motions.

233. (*First motion.*) Seize the cartridge box with the left hand, bend

Ground Arms.—No. 231.

the body, advance the left foot opposite the lower band, and seize the piece with the right hand.

234. (*Second motion.*) Raise the piece, bringing the left foot by the side of the right; turn the piece with the right hand, the rammer to the front; at the same time quit the cartridge box with the left hand, and drop this hand by the side.

Inspection of Arms.

235. The recruits being at *ordered arms*, and having the bayonet in the scabbard, if the instructor wishes to cause an inspection of arms, he will command:

Inspection—ARMS.

One time and two motions.

236. (*First motion.*) Seize the piece with the left hand below and near the upper band, carry it with both hands opposite the middle of the body, the butt between the feet, the rammer to the rear, the barrel vertical, the muzzle about three inches from the body; (should the rifle musket be used, the muzzle will be about eight inches from the body); carry the left hand reversed to the bayonet, draw it from the scabbard and fix it on the barrel; grasp the piece with the left hand below and near the upper band, seize the rammer with the thumb and fore-finger of the right hand bent, the other fingers closed.

237. (*Second motion.*) Draw the rammer as has been explained in *loading*, and let it glide to the bottom of the bore, replace the piece with the left hand opposite the right shoulder, and retake the position

of *ordered arms.*

238. The instructor will then inspect in succession the piece of each recruit, in passing along the front of the rank. Each, as the instructor reaches him, will raise smartly his piece with his right hand, seize it with the left between the lower band and guide sight, the lock to the front, the left hand at the height of the chin, the piece opposite to the left eye; the instructor will take it with the right hand at the handle, and, after inspecting it, will return it to the recruit, who will receive it back with the right hand, and replace it in the position of *ordered arms.*

239. When the instructor shall have passed him, each recruit will retake the position prescribed at the command *inspection*, return the rammer, *unfix the bayonet*, and resume the position of *ordered arms.*

240. If, instead of *inspection of arms*, the instructor should merely wish to cause bayonets to be fixed, he will command:

Fix—BAYONET.

241. Take the position indicated No. 236, fix bayonets as has been explained, and immediately resume the position of *ordered arms.*

242. If it be the wish of the instructor, after firing, to ascertain whether the pieces have been discharged, he will command:

Spring—RAMMERS.

243. Put the rammer in the barrel, as has been explained above, and immediately retake the position of *ordered arms.*

244. The instructor, for the purpose stated, can take the rammer by the small end, and spring it in the barrel, or cause each recruit to make it ring in the barrel.

245. Each recruit, after the instructor passes him, will return rammer, and resume the position of *ordered arms.*

Remarks on the Manual of Arms.

246. The manual of arms frequently distorts the persons of recruits before they acquire ease and confidence in the several positions. The instructor will therefore frequently recur to elementary principles in the course of the lessons.

247. Recruits are also extremely liable to curve the sides and back, and to derange the shoulders, especially in loading. Consequently, the instructor will not cause them to dwell too long at a time in one position.

248. When, after some days of exercise in the manual of arms, the four men shall be well established in their use, the instructor will al-

ways terminate the lesson by marching the men for some time in one rank, and at one pace apart, in common and quick time, in order to confirm them more and more in the mechanism of the step; he will also teach them to mark time, and to change step, which will be executed in the following manner:

To Mark Time.

249. The four men marching in the direct step, the instructor will command:

1. *Mark time.* 2. MARCH.

250. At the second command, which will be given at the instant a foot is coming to the ground, the recruits will make a semblance of marching, by bringing the heels by the side of each other, and observing the cadence of the step, by raising each foot alternately without advancing.

251. The instructor wishing the direct step to be resumed, will command:

1. *Forward*, 2. MARCH.

252. At the second command, which will be given as prescribed above, the recruits will retake the step of twenty-eight inches.

To Change Step.

253. The squad being in march, the instructor will command:

1. *Change step*, 2. MARCH.

254. At the second command, which will be given at the instant either foot is coming to the ground, bring the foot which is in rear by the side of that which is in front, and step off again with the foot which was in front.

To March Backward.

255. The instructor wishing the squad to march backward, will command:

1. *Squad backward*, 2. MARCH.

256. At the second command, the recruits will step off smartly with the left foot fourteen inches to the rear, reckoning from heel to heel, and so on with the feet in succession till the command *halt*, which will always be preceded by the caution *squad*. The men will halt at this command, and bring back the foot in front by the side of the other.

257. This step will always be executed in quick time.

258. The instructor will be watchful that the recruits march straight to the rear, and that the erect position of the body and the piece be

not deranged.

Lesson 3: To Load in Four Times.

259. The object of this lesson is to prepare the recruits to load at will, and to cause them to distinguish the times which require the greatest regularity and attention, such as *charge cartridge, ram cartridge,* and *prime.* It will be divided as follows:

260. The first time will be executed at the end of the command; the three others at the commands, *two, three* and *four.*

The instructor will command:

1. *Load in four times.* 2. LOAD.

261. Execute the times to include charge cartridge.

TWO.

262. Execute the times to include ram cartridge.

THREE.

263. Execute the times to include prime.

FOUR.

264. Execute the time of *shoulder arms.*

To Load at Will.

265. The instructor will next teach loading at will, which will he executed as loading in four times, but continued, and without resting on either of the times. He will command:

1. *Load at will,* 2. LOAD.

266. The instructor will habituate the recruits, by degrees, to load with the greatest possible promptitude, each without regulating himself by his neighbour, and above all without waiting for him.

267. The cadence prescribed No. 136, is not applicable to loading in four times, or at will.

Lesson 4: Firings.

268. The firings are direct or oblique, and will be executed as follows:

The Direct Fire.

269. The instructor will give the following commands:

1. *Fire by Squad.* 2. *Squad.* 3. READY. 4. AIM. 5. FIRE. 6. LOAD.

270. These several commands will be executed as has been prescribed in the *Manual of Arms.* At the third command, the men will come to the position of *ready,* as heretofore explained. At the fourth they will aim according to the rank in which each may find himself

placed, the rear-rank men inclining forward a little the upper part of the body, in order that their pieces may reach as much beyond the front rank as possible.

271. At the sixth command, they will load their pieces and return immediately to the position of *ready*.

272. The instructor will recommence the firing by the commands:
1. *Squad*. 2. AIM. 3. FIRE. 4. LOAD.

273. When the instructor wishes the firing to cease, he will command:

Cease—FIRING.

274. At this command the men will cease firing, but will load their pieces if unloaded, and afterward bring them to a shoulder.

Oblique Firings.

275. The oblique firings will be executed to the right and left, and by the same commands as the direct fire, with this single difference—the command *aim* will always be preceded by the caution, *right* or *left oblique*.

Position of the Two Ranks in the Oblique Fire to the Right.

276. At the command *ready*, the two ranks will execute what has been prescribed for the direct fire.

277. At the cautionary command, *right oblique*, the two ranks will throw back the right shoulder, and look steadily at the object to be hit.

278. At the command *aim*, each front-rank man will aim to the right without deranging the feet; each rear-rank man will advance the left foot about eight inches toward the right heel of the man next on the right of his file leader, and aim to the right, inclining the upper part of the body forward, and bending a little the left knee.

Position of the Two Ranks in the Oblique Fire to the Left.

279. At the cautionary command *left oblique*, the two ranks will throw back the left shoulder, and look steadily at the object to be hit.

280. At the command *aim*, the front rank will take aim to the left without deranging the feet; each man in the rear rank will advance the right foot about eight inches toward the right heel of the man next on the right of his file leader, and aim to the left, inclining the upper part of the body forward, and bending a little the right knee.

281. In both cases, at the command *load*, the men of each rank will come to the position of load as prescribed in the direct fire; the rear rank men bringing back the foot which is to the right and front by the

side of the other. Each man will continue to load as if isolated.

To Fire by File.

282. The fire by file will be executed by the two ranks, the files of which will fire successively, and without regulating on each other, except for the first fire.

283. The instructor will command:

1. *Fire by file.* 2. *Squad.* 3. READY. 4. COMMENCE FIRING.

284. At the third command, the two ranks will take the position prescribed in the direct fire.

285. At the fourth command, the file on the right will aim and fire; the rear-rank man in aiming will take the position indicated No. 183.

286. The men of this file will load their pieces briskly and fire a second time; reload and fire again, and so on in continuation.

287. The second file will aim, at the instant the first brings down pieces to reload, and will conform in all respects to that which has just been prescribed for the first file.

288. After the first fire, the front and rear rank men will not be required to fire at the same time,

289. Each man, after loading, will return to the position of *ready* and continue the fire.

290. When the instructor wishes the fire to cease, he will command:

Cease—FIRING.

291. At this command, the men will cease firing. If they have fired, they will load their pieces and bring them to a shoulder; if at the position of *ready*, they will half-cock and shoulder arms. If in the position of *aim*, they will bring down their pieces, half-cock, and shoulder arms.

To Fire by Rank.

292. The fire by rank will be executed by each entire rank, alternately.

293. The instructor will command:

1. *Fire by rank.* 2. *Squad.* 3. READY. 4. *Rear rank.*
5. AIM. 6. FIRE. 7. LOAD.

294. At the third command, the two ranks will take the position of *ready*, as prescribed in the direct fire.

295. At the seventh command, the rear rank will execute that which has been prescribed in the direct fire, and afterward take the

position of ready.

296. As soon as the instructor sees several men of the rear rank in the position of ready, he will command:

1. *Front rank.* 2. AIM. 3. FIRE. 4. LOAD.

297. At these commands, the men in the front rank will execute what has been prescribed for the rear rank, but they will not step off with the right foot.

298. The instructor will recommence the firing by the rear rank, and will thus continue to alternate from rank to rank, until he shall wish the firing to cease, when he will command, *cease firing*, which will be executed as heretofore prescribed.

Lesson 5: To Fire and Load Kneeling

299. In this exercise, the squad will be supposed loaded and drawn up in one rank. The instruction will be given to each man individually, without times or motions, and in the following manner:

300. The instructor will command:

FIRE and LOAD KNEELING.

301. At this command, the man on the right of the squad will move forward three paces and halt; then carry the right foot to the rear and to the right of the left heel, and in a position convenient for placing the right knee upon the ground in bending the left leg: place the right knee upon the ground; lower the piece, the left fore-arm supported upon the thigh on the same side, the right hand on the small of the stock, the butt resting on the right thigh, the left hand supporting the piece near the lower band.

To fire kneeling.—No. 301.

302. He will next move the right leg to the left around the knee supported on the ground, until this leg is nearly perpendicular to the direction of the left foot, and thus seat himself comfortably on the right heel.

303. Raise the piece with the right hand and support it with the left, holding it near the lower band, the left elbow resting on the left thigh near the knee; seize the hammer with the thumb, the fore-finger under the guard, cock and seize the piece at the small of the stock; bring the piece to the shoulder, *aim* and *fire*.

304. Bring the piece down as soon as it is fired, and support it with the left hand, the butt resting against the right thigh; carry the piece to the rear rising on the knee, the barrel downward, the butt resting on the ground; in this position support the piece with the left hand at the upper band, draw cartridge with the right and load the piece, ramming the ball, if necessary, with both hands.

305. When loaded bring the piece to the front with the left hand, which holds it at the upper band; seize it at the same time with the right hand at the small of the stock; turn the piece, the barrel uppermost and nearly horizontal, the left elbow resting on the left thigh; half cock, remove the old cap and prime, rise, and return to the ranks.

306. The second man will then be taught what has just been prescribed for the first, and so on through the remainder of the squad.

To Fire and Load Lying.

307. In this exercise the squad will be in one rank and loaded; the instruction will be given individually and without times or motions.

308. The instructor will command:

FIRE and LOAD LYING.

309. At this command, the man on the right of the squad will move forward three paces and halt; he will then bring his piece to an order, drop on both knees, and place himself on the ground flat on his belly. In this position he will support the piece nearly horizontal with the left hand, holding it near the lower band, the butt end of the piece and the left elbow resting on the ground, the barrel uppermost; cock the piece with the right hand, and carry this hand to the small of the stock; raise the piece with both hands, press the butt against the shoulder, and, resting on both elbows, *aim* and *fire*.

310. As soon as he has fired, bring the piece down and turn upon his left side, still resting on his left elbow; bring back the piece until the cock is opposite his breast, the butt end resting on the ground;

take out a cartridge with the right hand; seize the small of the stock with this hand, holding the cartridge with the thumb and two first fingers; he will then throw himself on his back, still holding the piece with both hands; carry the piece to the rear, place the butt between the heels, the barrel up, the muzzle elevated. In this position, charge cartridge, draw rammer, ram cartridge, and return rammer.

311. When finished loading, the man will turn again upon his left side, remove the old cap and prime, then raise the piece vertically, rise, turn about, and resume his position in the ranks.

312. The second man will be taught what has just been prescribed for the first, and so on throughout the squad.

Lesson 6: Bayonet Exercise.

313. The bayonet exercise in this book will be confined to two movements, the *guard against infantry*, and the *guard against cavalry*. The men will be placed in one rank, with two paces interval, and, being at shoulder arms, the instructor will command:

1. *Guard against Infantry.* 2. GUARD.
One time and two motions.

314. (*First motion.*) Make a half face to the right, turning on both heels, the feet square to each other; at the same time raise the piece slightly, and seize it with the left; hand above and near the lower band.

315. (*Second motion.*) Carry the right foot twenty inches perpendicularly to the rear, the right heel on the prolongation of the left, the knees slightly bent, the weight of the body resting equally on both legs; lower the piece with both hands, the barrel uppermost, the left elbow against the body; seize the piece at the same time with the right hand at the small of the stock, the arms falling naturally, the point of the bayonet slightly elevated.

Shoulder—ARMS.
One time and one motion,

316. Throw up the piece with the left hand, and place it against the right shoulder, at the same time bring the right heel by the side of the left and face to the front.

1. *Guard against Cavalry.* 2. GUARD.
One time and two motions.

317. Both motions the same as for guard against infantry, except that the right hand will be supported against the hip, and the bayonet held at the height of the eye, as in charge bayonet.

Shoulder—ARMS.

Guard against Infantry.—No. 314.

Guard against Cavalry.—No. 317.

One time and one motion.

318. Spring up the piece with the left hand and place it against the right shoulder, at the same time bring the right heel by the side of the left, and face to the front.

Part Third

319. When the recruits are well established in the *principles and mechanism of the step, the position of the body, and the manual of arms,* the instructor will unite eight men, at least, and twelve men at most, in order to teach them the principles of alignment, the principles of the touch of elbows in marching to the front, the principles of the march by the flank, wheeling from a halt, wheeling in marching, and the change of direction to the side of the guide. He will place the squad in one rank, elbow to elbow, and number the men from right to left.

Lesson 1: Alignments,

320. The instructor will at first teach the recruits to align themselves, man by man, in order the better to make them comprehend the principles of alignment; to this end, he will command the two men on the right flank to march two paces to the front, and having aligned them, he will caution the remainder of the squad to move up, as they may be successively called, each by his number, and align themselves successively on the line of the first two men.

321. Each recruit, as designated by his number will turn the head and eyes to the right, as prescribed in the first lesson of the first part, and will march in *quick time two paces forward,* shortening the last, so as to find himself about six inches behind the new alignment, which he ought never to pass: he will next move up steadily by steps of two or three inches, the hams extended, to the side of the man next to him on the alignment, so that, without deranging the head, the line of the eyes, or that of the shoulders, he may find himself in the exact line of his neighbour, whose elbow he will lightly touch without opening his own.

322. The instructor seeing the rank well aligned, will command:
FRONT.

323. At this, the recruits will turn eyes to the front, and remain firm.

324. Alignments to the left will be executed on the same principles.

325. When the recruits shall have thus learned to align themselves, man by man, correctly, and without groping or jostling, the instructor

will cause the entire rank to align itself at once by the command:

Right (or *left*)—DRESS.

326. At this the rank, except the two men placed in advance as a basis of alignment, will move up in quick time, and place themselves on the new line, according to the principles prescribed No. 321.

327. The instructor, placed five or six paces in front, and facing the rank, will carefully observe that the principles are followed, and then pass to the flank that has served as a basis, to verify the alignment.

328. The instructor, seeing the greater number of the rank aligned, will command

FRONT.

329. The instructor may afterward order *this* or *that* file *forward* or *back*, designating each by its number. The file or files designated, only, will slightly turn the head toward the basis, to judge how much they ought to move up or back, steadily place themselves on the line, and then turn eyes to the front, without a particular command to that effect.

330. Alignments to the rear will be executed on the same principles, the recruits stepping back a little beyond the line, and then dressing up according to the principles prescribed No. 321, the instructor commanding:

Right (or *left*) *backward*—DRESS.

331. After each alignment, the instructor will examine the position of the men, and cause the rank to come to *ordered arms*, to prevent too much fatigue, and also the danger of negligence at shouldered arms.

Lessor 2

332. The men having learned, in the first and second parts to march with steadiness in common time, and to take steps equal in length and swiftness, will be exercised in the third part only in *quick time, double quick time* and the *run*; the instructor will cause them to execute successively, at these different gaits, the march to the front, the facing about in marching, the march by the flank, the wheels at a halt and in marching, and the changes of direction to the side of the guide.

333. The instructor will inform the recruits that at the command *march*, they will always move off in *quick time*, unless this command should be preceded by that of *double quick*.

To March to the Front.

334. The rank being correctly aligned, when the instructor shall

wish to cause it to march by the front, he will place a well instructed man on the right or the left, according to the side on which he may wish the guide to be, and command:

1. *Squad, forward.* 2. *Guide right* (or *left*). 3. MARCH.

335. At the command *march*, the rank will step off smartly with the left foot; the guide will take care to march straight to the front, keeping his shoulders always in a square with that line.

333. The instructor will observe, in marching to the front, that the men touch lightly the elbow toward the side of the guide; that they do not open out the left elbow, nor the right arm; that they yield to pressure coming from the side of the guide, and resist that coming from the opposite side; that they recover by insensible degrees the slight touch of the elbow, if lost; that they maintain the head direct to the front, no matter on which side the guide may be; and if found before or behind the alignment, that the man in fault corrects himself by shortening or lengthening the step, by degrees, almost insensible.

337. The instructor will labour to cause recruits to comprehend that the alignment can only be preserved, in marching, by the regularity of the step, the touch of the elbow, and the maintenance of the shoulders in a square with the line of direction: that if, for example, the step of some be longer than that of others, or if some march faster than others, a separation of elbows, and a loss of the alignment, would be inevitable; that if (it being required that the head should be direct to the front) they do not strictly observe the touch of elbows, it would be impossible for an individual to judge whether he marches abreast with his neighbour, or not, and whether there be not an interval between them.

338. The impulsion of the quick step having a tendency to make men too easy and tree in their movements, the instructor will be careful to regulate the cadence of this step, and to habituate them to preserve always the erectness of the body, and the due length of the pace.

339. The men being well established in the principles of the direct march; the instructor will exercise them in marching obliquely. The rank being in march, the instructor will command:

1. *Right* (or *left*) *oblique.* 2. MARCH.

340. At the second command, each man will make a half face to the right (or left), and will then march straight-forward in the new direction. As the men no longer touch elbows, they will glance along the shoulders of the nearest files, toward the side to which they are obliquing, and will regulate their steps so that the shoulder shall always

be behind that of their next neighbour on that side, and that his head shall conceal the heads of the other men in the rank. Besides this, the men should preserve the same length of pace, and the same degree of obliquity.

341. The instructor wishing to resume the primitive direction, will command:

1. *Forward.* 2. MARCH.

342. At the second command, each man will make a half face to the left (or right), and all will then march straight to the front, conforming to the principles of the direct march.

To March to the Front in Double Quick Time.

343. When the several principles, heretofore explained, have become familiar to the recruits, and they shall be well established in the position of the body, the bearing of arms, and the mechanism, length, and swiftness of the step, the instructor will pass them from *quick* to *double quick* time, and the reverse, observing not to make them march obliquely in double quick time, till they are well established in the cadence of this step.

344. The squad being at a march in quick time, the instructor will command:

1. *Double quick.* 2. MARCH.

345. At the command *march*, which will be given when either foot is coming to the ground, the squad will step off in double quick time. The men will endeavour to follow the principles laid down in the first part of this book, and to preserve the alignment.

346. When the instructor wishes the squad to resume the step in quick time, he will command:

1. *Quick time*, 2. MARCH.

347. At the command *march*, which will be given when either foot is coming to the ground, the squad will retake the step in quick time.

348. The squad being in march, the instructor will halt it by the commands and means prescribed Nos. 105 and 106. The command *halt*, will be given an instant before the foot is ready to be placed on the ground.

349. The squad being in march in double quick time, the instructor will occasionally cause it to mark time by the commands prescribed No. 249. The men will then mark double quick time, without altering the cadence of the step. He will also cause them to pass from the direct to the oblique step, and reciprocally, conforming to what has

been prescribed No. 339, and following.

350. The squad being at a halt, the instructor will cause it to march in double quick time, by preceding the command *march*, by *double quick*.

351. The instructor will endeavour to regulate well the cadence of the step.

To Face About in Marching.

352. If the squad be marching in quick, or double quick time, and the instructor should wish to march it in retreat, he will command:

1. *Squad right about.* 2. MARCH.

353. At the command *march*, which will be given at the instant the left foot is coming to the ground, the recruit will bring this foot to the ground, and turning on it, will face to the rear; he will then place the right foot in the new direction, and step off with the left foot.

354. If the instructor should wish merely to face the squad about, without marching it in retreat, he will command:

1. *Squad right about.* 2. HALT.

355. At the command *halt*, which will be given the instant the left foot is coming to the ground, the recruit will face about as prescribed No. 353; he will then place the right foot by the side of the left.

To March Backward.

356. The squad being at a halt, if the instructor should wish to march it in the back step, he will command:

1. *Squad backward.* 2. *Guide left* (or *right*.) 3. MARCH.

357. The back step will be executed by the means prescribed No. 256.

358. The instructor, in this step, will be watchful that the men do not lean on each other.

359. As the march to the front in quick time should only be executed at shouldered arms, the instructor, in order not to fatigue the men too much, and also to prevent negligence in gait and position, will halt the squad from time to time, and cause arms to be ordered.

360. In marching at *double quick time*, the men will always carry their pieces on the *right shoulder* or at a *trail*. *This rule is general.*

361. If the instructor shall wish the pieces carried at a trail he will give the command *trail* arms, before the command *double quick*. If, on the contrary, this command be not given, the men will shift their pieces to the right shoulder at the command *double quick*. In either

case, at the command *halt*, the men will bring their pieces to the position of *shoulder arms*. *This rule is general*.

Lesson 3: The March by the Flank

362. The rank being at a halt, and correctly aligned, the instructor will command:

1. Squad., right—FACE. 2. *Forward*, 3. MARCH.

363. At the last part of the first command, the rank will face to the right; the even numbered men, after facing to the right, will step quickly to the right side of the odd numbered men, the latter standing fast, so that when the movement is executed, the men will be formed into files of two men abreast.

364. At the third command, the squad will step off smartly with the left foot; the files keeping aligned, and preserving their intervals.

365. The march by the left flank will be executed by the same commands, substituting the word *left* for *right*., and by inverse means; in this case, the even numbered men, after facing to the left will stand fast, and the odd numbered will place themselves on their left.

366. The instructor will place a well instructed soldier by the side of the recruit who is at the head of the rank, to regulate the step, and to conduct him; and it will be enjoined on this recruit to march always elbow to elbow with the soldier.

367. The instructor will cause to be observed in the march, by the flank, the following rules:

That the step be executed according to the principles prescribed for the direct step;

Because these principles, without which men placed elbow to elbow, in the same rank, cannot preserve unity and harmony of movement, are of a more necessary observance in marching in file.

That the head of the man who immediately precedes, covers the heads of all who are in front;

Because it is the most certain rule by which each man may maintain himself in the exact line of the file.

368. The instructor will place himself habitually five or six paces on the flank of the rank marching in file, to watch over the execution of the principles prescribed above. He will also place himself sometimes in its rear, halt, and suffer it to pass fifteen or twenty paces, the better to see whether the men cover each other accurately.

369. When he shall wish to halt the rank, marching by the flank, and to cause it to face to the front, he will command:

1. *Squad*, 2. HALT. 3. FRONT.

370. At the second command, the rank will halt, and afterward no man will stir, although he may have lost his distance. This prohibition is necessary, to habituate the men to a constant preservation of their distances.

371. At the third command, each man will front by facing to the left, if marching by the right flank, and by a face to the right, if marching by the left flank. The rear-rank men will at the same time move quickly into their places, so as to form the squad again into one rank.

372. When the men have become accustomed to marching by the flank, the instructor will cause them to change direction by file; for this purpose, he will command:

1. *By file left* (or *right*). 2. MARCH.

373. At the command *march*, the first file will change direction to the left (or right) in describing a small arc of a circle, and will then march straight-forward; the two men of this file, in wheeling, will keep up the touch of the elbows, and the man on the side to which the wheel is made, will shorten the first three or four steps. Each file will come successively to wheel on the same spot where that which preceded it wheeled.

374. The instructor will also cause the squad to face by the right or left flank in marching, and for this purpose will command:

1. *Squad by the right* (or *left*) *flank*. 2. MARCH.

375. At the second command, which will be given a little before either foot comes to the ground, the recruits will turn the body, plant the foot that is raised in the new direction, and step off with the other foot without altering the cadence of the step; the men will double or undouble rapidly.

376. If in facing by the right or the left flank, the squad should face to the rear, the men will come into one rank, agreeably to the principles indicated No. 371. It is to be remarked, that it is the men who are in the rear who always move up to form into single rank, and in such manner as never to invert the order of the numbers in the rank.

377. If, when the squad has been faced to the rear, the instructor should cause it to face by the left flank, it is the even numbers who will double by moving to the left of the odd numbers; but if by the right flank, it is the odd numbers who will double to the right of the even numbers.

378. This lesson, like the preceding one, will be practised with pieces at a shoulder; but the instructor may, to give relief by change,

occasionally order *support arms,* and he will require of the recruits marching in this position as much regularity as in the former.

379. If the instructor should wish merely to face the squad by the flank, without marching forward, he will command:

1. Squad by the right (or *left*) *flank*, 2. HALT.

380. At the command *halt*, the recruit will face as prescribed. No. 375; he will then place the foot that is raised by the side of the other.

The March by the Flank in Double Quick Time.

381. The principles of the march by the flank in double quick time, are the same as in quick time. The instructor will give the commands prescribed No. 362, taking care always to give the command *double quick* before that of *march.*

382. He will pay the greatest attention to the cadence of the step.

383. The instructor will cause the change of direction, and the march by the flank, to be executed in double quick time, by the same commands, and according to the same principles, as in quick time.

384. The instructor will cause the pieces to be carried either on the *right shoulder* or at a *trail.*

385. The instructor will sometimes march the squad by the flank, without doubling the files.

383. The principles of this march are the same as in two ranks, and it will always be executed in quick time.

387. The instructor will give the commands prescribed, No. 362, but he will be careful to caution the squad not to double files.

388. The instructor will be watchful that the men do not bend their knees unequally, which would cause them to tread on the heels of the men in front, and also to lose the cadence of the step and their distances.

389. The various movements in this lesson will be executed in single rank. In the changes of direction, the leading man will change direction without altering the length or the cadence of the step. The instructor will recall to the attention of the men, that in facing by the right or left flank in marching, they will not double, but march in one rank.

Lesson 4: Wheelings.

General Principles of Wheeling.

390. Wheelings are of two kinds: from halts, or on fixed pivots, and in march, or on movable pivots.

391. Wheeling on a fixed pivot takes place in passing a corps from the order in battle to the order in column, or from the latter to the former.

392. Wheels in marching take place in changes of direction in column, as often as this movement is executed to the side opposite to the guide.

393. In wheels from a halt, the pivot-man only turns in his place, without advancing or receding.

394. In the wheels in marching, the pivot takes steps of nine or eleven inches, according as the squad is marching in quick or double quick time, so as to clear the wheeling-point, which is necessary, in order that the subdivisions of a column may change direction without losing their distances, as will be explained in the School of the Company.

395. the man on the wheeling-flank will take the fall step of twenty-eight inches, or thirty-three inches, according to the gait.

WHEELING FROM A HALT, OR ON A FIXED PIVOT.

396. The rank being at a halt, the instructor will place a well-instructed man on the wheeling-flank to conduct it, and then command:

1. *By squad, right wheel.* 2. MARCH.

397. At the second command, the rank will step off with the left foot, turning at the same time the head a little to the left, the eyes fixed on the line of the eyes of the men to their left; the pivot-man will merely mark time in gradually turning his body, in order to conform himself to the movement of the marching flank; the man who conducts this flank will take steps of twenty-eight inches, and from the first step advance a little the left shoulder, cast his eyes from time to time along the rank, and feel constantly the elbow of the next man lightly, but never push him.

398. The other men will feel lightly the elbow of the next man toward the pivot, resist pressure coming from the opposite side, and each will conform himself to the marching flank—shortening his step according to his approximation to the pivot.

399. The instructor will make the rank wheel round the circle once or twice before halting, in order to cause the principles to be the better understood, and he will be watchful that the centre does not break.

400. He will cause the wheel to the left to be executed according

to the same principles.

401. When the instructor shall wish to arrest the wheel, he will command:

1. *Squad.* 2. HALT.

402. At the second command, the rank will halt, and no man stir. The instructor, going to the flank opposite the pivot, will place the two outer men of that flank in the direction he may wish to give to the rank, without however displacing the pivot, who will conform the line of his shoulders to this direction. The instructor will take care to have between these two men, and the pivot, only the space necessary to contain the other men. He will then command;

Left (or *right*)—DRESS.

403. At this, the rank will place itself on the alignment of the two men established as the basis, in conformity with the principles prescribed.

404. The instructor will next command: FRONT, which will be executed as prescribed No. 323.

REMARKS ON THE PRINCIPLES OF THE WHEEL FROM A HALT.

405. *Turn a little the head toward the marching flank, and fix the eyes on the line of the eyes of the men who are on that side;*

Because, otherwise, it would be impossible for each man to regulate the length of his step so as to conform his own movement to that of the marching flank.

Touch lightly the elbow of the next man toward the pivot;
In order that the files may not open out in the wheel.

Resist pressure that comes from the side of the marching flank;
Because, if this principle be neglected, the pivot, which ought to be a fixed point, in wheels from a halt, might be pushed out of its place by pressure.

WHEELING IN MARCHING, OR ON A MOVABLE PIVOT.

406. When the recruits have been brought to execute well the wheel from a halt, they will be taught to wheel in marching.

407. To this end, the rank being in march, when the instructor shall wish to cause it to change direction to the reverse flank (to the side opposite to the guide or pivot flank), he will command:

1. *Right* (or *left*) *wheel.* 2. MARCH.

408. The first command will be given when the rank is yet *four* paces from the wheeling point.

409, At the second command, the wheel will be executed in the same manner as from a halt, except that the touch of the elbow will remain toward the marching flank (or side of the guide) instead of the side of the actual pivot; that the pivot man, instead of merely turning in his place, will conform himself to the movement of the marching flank, feel lightly the elbow of the next man, take steps of full nine inches, and thus gain ground forward in describing a small curve so as to clear the point of the wheel. The middle of the rank will bend slightly to the rear. As soon as the movement shall commence, the man who conducts the marching flank will cast his eyes on the ground over which he will have to pass.

410. The wheel being ended, the instructor will command:

1. *Forward.* 2. March.

411, The first command will be pronounced when *four* paces are yet required to complete the change of direction.

412. At the command *march*, which will be given at the instant of completing the wheel, the man who conducts the marching flank will direct himself straight-forward; the pivot man and all the rank will retake the step of twenty-eight inches, and bring the head direct to the front.

TURNING, OR CHANGE OF DIRECTION TO THE SIDE OF THE GUIDE.

413. The change of direction to the side of the guide, in marching, will be executed as follows: The instructor will command:

1. *Left* (or *right*) *turn.* 2. MARCH.

414. The first command will be given when the rank is yet *four* paces from the turning point.

415. At the command *march*, to be pronounced at the instant the rank ought to turn, the guide will face to the left (or right) in marching, and move forward in the new direction without slackening or quickening the cadence, and without shortening or lengthening the step. The whole rank will promptly conform itself to the new direction: to effect which, each man will advance the shoulder opposite to the guide, take the double quick step, to carry himself in the new direction, turn the head and eyes to the side of the guide, and retake the touch of the elbow on that side, in placing himself on the alignment of the guide, from whom he will take the step, and then resume the direct position of the head. Each man will thus arrive successively on the alignment.

WHEELING AND CHANGING DIRECTION TO THE SIDE OF THE

Guide, in Double Quick Time.

416. When the recruits comprehend and execute well, in quick time, the wheels at a halt and in marching, and the change of direction to the side of the guide, the instructor will cause the same movements to be repeated in double quick time.

417. These various movements will be executed by the same commands and according to the same principles as in quick time, except that, the command *double quick*, will precede that of march. In wheeling while marching, the pivot man will take steps of eleven inches, and in the changes of direction to the side of the guide, the men on the side opposite the guide must increase the gait in order to bring themselves into line.

418. The instructor, in order not to fatigue the recruits, and not to divide their attention, will cause them to execute the several movements of which this lesson is composed, first without arms, and next, after the mechanism be well comprehended, with arms.

Lesson 5: Long Marches in Double Quick Time and the Run.

419. The instructor will cause to be resumed the exercises in double quick time and the run, with arms and knapsacks.

420, He will cause long marches to be executed in double quick time, both by the front and by the flank, and by constant practice will lead the men to pass over a distance of five miles in sixty minutes. The pieces will be carried on either shoulder, and sometimes at a trail.

421. He will also exercise them in long marches at a run, the pieces carried at will; the men will be instructed to keep as united as possible, without however exacting much regularity, which is impracticable.

422. The run, in actual service, will only be resorted to when it may be highly important to reach a given point with great promptitude.

To Stack Arms.

The men being at order arms with bayonets unfixed, the instructor will command:

Stack—ARMS.

423. At this command, the front-rank man of every even-numbered file will pass his piece before him, seizing it with the left hand near the upper band; will place the butt a little in advance of his left toe, the barrel turned toward the body, and draw the rammer slightly from its place; the front-rank man of every odd numbered file will also draw

the rammer slightly, and pass his piece to the man next on his left, who will seize it with the right hand near the upper band, and place the butt a little in advance of the right toe of the man next on his right, the barrel turned to the front; he will then cross the rammers of the two pieces, the rammer of the piece of the odd numbered man being inside; the rear rank man of every even file will also draw his rammer, lean his piece forward, the lock-plate downwards, advance the right foot about six inches, and insert the rammer between the rammer and barrel of the piece of his front-rank man; with his left hand he will place the butt of his piece on the ground, thirty-two inches in rear of, and perpendicular to, the front rank, bringing back his right foot by the side of the left; the front-rank man of every even file will at the same time lean the stack to the rear, quit it with his right hand, and force all the rammers down. The stack being thus formed, the rear-rank man of every odd file will pass his piece into his left hand, the barrel to the front, and inclining it forward, will rest it on the stack.

424, If the rifle musket be used and it is required to stack arms with the bayonets fixed, the following will be the method.

425, At the command *stack arms*, the front-rank man of every even-numbered file will pass his piece before him, seizing it with the left hand above the middle band, and place the butt behind and near the right foot of the man next on the left, the barrel turned to the front. At the same time the front-rank man of every odd-numbered file will pass his piece before him, seizing it with the left hand below the middle band, and hand it to the man next on the left; the latter will receive it with the right hand two inches above the middle band, throw the butt about thirty-two inches to the front, opposite to his right shoulder, inclining the muzzle toward him, and lock the shanks of the two bayonets: the lock of this second piece toward the right, and its shank above that of the first piece. The rear-rank man of every even file will project his bayonet forward, and introduce it (using both hands) between and under the shanks of the two other bayonets. He will then abandon the piece to his file leader, who will receive it with the right hand under the middle band, bring the butt to the front, holding up his own piece and the stack with the left hand, and place the butt of this third piece between the feet of the man next on the right, the S plate to the rear. The stack thus formed, the rear-rank man of every odd file will pass his piece into his left hand, the barrel turned to the front, and, sloping the bayonet forward, rest it on the stack.

426. The men of both ranks having taken the position of the sol-

dier without arms, the instructor will command:

1. *Break ranks.* 2. MARCH.

To Resume Arms.

427. Both ranks being re-formed in rear of their stacks, the instructor will command:

Take—ARMS.

428. At this command, the rear-rank man of every odd-numbered file will withdraw his piece from the stack; the front-rank man of every even file will seize his own piece with the left hand and that of the man on his right with his right hand, both above the lower band; the rear-rank man of the even file will seize his piece with the right hand below the lower band (if the rifle musket be used the piece will be seized at the middle band); these two men will raise up the stack to loosen the rammers, or shanks of the bayonets. The front-rank man of every odd file will facilitate the disengagement of the rammers, if necessary, by drawing them out slightly with the left hand, and will receive his piece from the hand of the man next on his left; the four men will retake the position of the soldier at order arms.

ALSO FROM LEONAUR
AVAILABLE IN SOFTCOVER OR HARDCOVER WITH DUST JACKET

THE FALL OF THE MOGHUL EMPIRE OF HINDUSTAN *by H. G. Keene*—By the beginning of the nineteenth century, as British and Indian armies under Lake and Wellesley dominated the scene, a little over half a century of conflict brought the Moghul Empire to its knees.

LADY SALE'S AFGHANISTAN *by Florentia Sale*—An Indomitable Victorian Lady's Account of the Retreat from Kabul During the First Afghan War.

THE CAMPAIGN OF MAGENTA AND SOLFERINO 1859 *by Harold Carmichael Wylly*—The Decisive Conflict for the Unification of Italy.

FRENCH'S CAVALRY CAMPAIGN *by J. G. Maydon*—A Special Correspondent's View of British Army Mounted Troops During the Boer War.

CAVALRY AT WATERLOO *by Sir Evelyn Wood*—British Mounted Troops During the Campaign of 1815.

THE SUBALTERN *by George Robert Gleig*—The Experiences of an Officer of the 85th Light Infantry During the Peninsular War.

NAPOLEON AT BAY, 1814 *by F. Loraine Petre*—The Campaigns to the Fall of the First Empire.

NAPOLEON AND THE CAMPAIGN OF 1806 *by Colonel Vachée*—The Napoleonic Method of Organisation and Command to the Battles of Jena & Auerstädt.

THE COMPLETE ADVENTURES IN THE CONNAUGHT RANGERS *by William Grattan*—The 88th Regiment during the Napoleonic Wars by a Serving Officer.

BUGLER AND OFFICER OF THE RIFLES *by William Green & Harry Smith*—With the 95th (Rifles) during the Peninsular & Waterloo Campaigns of the Napoleonic Wars.

NAPOLEONIC WAR STORIES *by Sir Arthur Quiller-Couch*—Tales of soldiers, spies, battles & sieges from the Peninsular & Waterloo campaingns.

CAPTAIN OF THE 95TH (RIFLES) *by Jonathan Leach*—An officer of Wellington's sharpshooters during the Peninsular, South of France and Waterloo campaigns of the Napoleonic wars.

RIFLEMAN COSTELLO *by Edward Costello*—The adventures of a soldier of the 95th (Rifles) in the Peninsular & Waterloo Campaigns of the Napoleonic wars.

AVAILABLE ONLINE AT **www.leonaur.com**
AND FROM ALL GOOD BOOK STORES

www.ingramcontent.com/pod-product-compliance
Lightning Source LLC
Chambersburg PA
CBHW032122090426
42743CB00007B/427